The Princeton Review®

PrincetonReview.com

The Portable Guidance Counselor

Answers to the 284 Most Important Questions About Getting Into College

By the Staff of The Princeton Review

Random House, Inc.
New York

The Princeton Review, Inc.
2315 Broadway
New York, NY 10024
E-mail: editorialsupport@review.com

ISBN: 978-0-375-42936-1

VP, Publisher: Robert Franek
AVP, Production: Scott Harris
Editors: Laura Braswell and Adam Davis
Production Editor: Kristen O'Toole

Printed in the United States of America on partially recycled paper.

9 8 7 6 5 4 3 2 1

Acknowledgements

This book was the result of months of preparation, execution, collection, and assembly, so it goes without saying (yet I'm saying it anyway) that it couldn't have been done without the effort of many talented individuals.

First and foremost, I'd like to thank all the counselors who took time out of their busy schedules to fill out the survey that yielded the many hundred quotes you'll find on the following pages—each and every one of them was instrumental in shaping this book, and their expertise and candor was (and still are) deeply appreciated.

Thanks are also due to my steadfast team of writers: Kerry Dexter, Elizabeth Faith, Naomi Rockler-Gladen, Landon Hall, Tom Haushalter, Michael Palumbo, and Kelly Smith—their fine work with the written word made mine all the easier.

Also, thank you to Kim Howie, Scott Harris, and Kristen O'Toole for proving themselves, as always, to be a design and production team par excellence. Thanks, too, to David Soto and Ben Zelevansky for their speedy work in the mysterious underworld of surveys.

Finally, I'd like to thank Rob Franek and Seamus Mullarkey for their guidance and vision, and most of all, thanks to the readers of this book—I hope you find everything hereafter to be more than useful in your college searches and applications. Good luck and keep learning.

—Adam Davis

December 2009

TABLE OF CONTENTS

Introduction

A Word Before Your First Steps on the Road to College . . .

A long time ago, shortly after dinosaurs ceased walking the Earth, going to college after high school was a thing of rare privilege. Most likely, the only people who could seek out higher education were those of such a financially abundant background that they had little need to work and all the time in the world to study. Times, needless to say, have changed.

Nowadays, it's become more and more rare for high school graduates not to head directly to college—in a way, it's expected of them, and with the allure of independence and fun (along with a few challenging classes) they seem more than happy to go. Yet the process, while extremely rewarding, has gone from cut-and-dry to a virtual swampland of questions, forms, money, and confusion. And with more students than ever before going to college, school counselors find themselves spread thin when it comes to guiding them along the road to college. That's where this book comes in.

To give you an idea of what you'll be facing, take a look at these stats taken from The Princeton Review's 2009 College Hopes &

Worries Survey, which asked students and parents nationwide a series of questions about their feelings regarding the college admissions process. We received 10,388 responses (8,776 high school students applying to colleges and 1,612 parents of college applicants) and arrived at the following numbers.

When asked how they would gauge their stress level about the college application process, 43 percent of students and parents alike replied "high."

When asked how they would rate the amount of information and support they've received from their school guidance counselor to help them through their college applications for admission and financial aid, 31 percent of students and 30 percent of parents said they found the support "adequate."

When asked what has been (or what they think will be) the toughest part of the college application experience, 32 percent of students said "deciding which college to attend," while 31 percent of parents said "writing college essays and completing applications."

When asked what their biggest concern about applying to or attending college will be, 37 percent of students and 34 percent of parents said they were worried they "will get into first-choice college, but won't have sufficient funds/financial aid to attend."

There you have it. Students have questions. Parents have questions. Colleges have questions about the students. And between all this are the school counselors, working diligently to assuage everyone's fears—and now there's **The Portable Guidance Counselor,** a book crafted by culling only the most informative answers from counselors themselves to the most important questions college applicants face. In order to do this, The Princeton Review created a survey that asked 100 of the most important questions high school students face when it comes to college. We then gave that survey to more than 2,500 counselors worldwide to see what they had to say. Receiving their replies, we went through each and every response to garner the information that fills this book. Truth be told, it was no easy job, but we feel that it has illuminated every corner of the college admissions process. From middle school to your first tuition payment, you'll find everything you need to know here.

Start with Chapter 1 to see what you can do in high school to become the strongest applicant possible, and learn how to best go about every facet of your college search. Then on to Chapter 2 to find out how much your grades, extracurriculars, and other personal items will count at the college admissions office. Chapter 3 gives you all you need to know about applying to college with no stone or question unturned so that you'll know exactly what you'll need to do and how to do it. After sending out your application, the next step is waiting for that special envelope—or envelopes—in the mail, and that's where Chapter 4 comes in, with helpful information on how to handle the interview and what to do if you're accepted, waitlisted, or denied. Finally, Chapter 5 allows you to look at the whole process from a counselor's point of view. What are their greatest success stories? Their biggest defeats? What do they wish students would do more often and what advice do they have for them in order to stay ahead of the game?

As helpful, in our humble opinion, as this book is, it's best used in conjunction with your parents, your friends and teachers and, most of all, your counselor. Explore your questions both here and with them in person. Maybe this will fill in some blanks after meeting with them. Maybe vice-versa. You can also visit PrincetonReview.com for tips and advice. There you'll also find our "Eye on Apply," where we check in with a diverse group of high school seniors as they navigate their way through the college admissions process, giving an inside perspective on picking schools, visiting campuses, writing essays, filling out applications, and more. It's a great way to get a clear view of what you'll be facing come college admissions time. Either way, the best thing you can do to enhance the likelihood of you being accepted at your best fit college is to be as informed as possible. It's no joke or GI Joe moral: Knowledge is power. And in this situation, it's not just half the battle, it's the whole battle.

So good luck and keep your chin up—the college application process was never meant to be fun, but that doesn't mean it has to be stressful or difficult. Ask for help when you need it and stay focused on the end result—college! We've been right where you are, so trust us when we say all your hard work will be more than worth it.

Chapter 1
What to Consider When Considering Colleges

READY, SET, WHEN?!

When should I start thinking about the college admissions process?

Kiko, 8th grader, New Mexico, plays softball, and she wants to go to a "green" school

Some students dream of careers that require college degrees while others don't know what they want to be when they grow up even after they've grown up. Whether you asked for a stethoscope when you were six years old and have always seen college as part of your future, or whether you aren't yet sure what you want out of your education, college counselors agree that it's a good idea to keep your options open, which means planning your education early. You don't want to cut off possibilities and end up wasting time and money while wandering down a wrong course.

Birth?
Many college counselors advise parents to start the process of college admissions really early. Lead counselor Ellen E. Underwood says, "Thinking about college should be encouraged by parents from the cradle. Stick a pacifier and bib from your favorite school on that kid! There is no such thing as starting too early!"

Grade school?
Counselor Tracie Morrison shares the perspective that earlier is better: "The admissions process begins as soon as a student decides to attend college after graduation. From the moment a child receives a first grade in school, thinking about college should begin. I say this because if you have a long-term goal of attending college, every decision you make from that moment on becomes pertinent to the end result."

Junior high?
While it is true that it's never too early to start preparing, decisions that impact the college applications process actually begin to emerge in about the 8th grade. Counselor Steven Newton says, "Junior high school is a great time

to dream of careers and to begin the research of how to get there." From a pragmatic point of view, counselor Bruce A. Smith explains that "8th grade grades often affect course selection in 9th grade." He adds, "Good grades open up more options for you, and the key to a successful high school experience is to keep as many options open as possible." For example, some competitive colleges may strongly prefer students who take four years of foreign language in high school. If you don't choose wisely when registering for high school classes, you may cut yourself off from the possibility of attending certain colleges. Independent counselor Valerie Broughton says, "When students are choosing their courses in 8th or 9th grade, their choices either leave doors to colleges open to them, or their choices close some options." This means that students who have their eyes on the most selective schools should begin making educational choices early on, at least by freshman year of high school.

As a freshman or sophomore?

Many counselors cite the freshman and sophomore years of high school as an important time to begin the preliminary stages of college planning. Bill Kellerman, an educational consultant, says that freshman year of high school is a good time for "plotting out coursework and extracurricular plans-of-action that remain flexible and achievable." Shirley Bloomquist, an independent college counselor, agrees. She says, "I like to have one to two meetings with freshmen in order to review academic success strategies, to discuss a challenging course load (but not one that is overwhelming), and to discuss extracurricular goals and summer plans."

Though freshman and sophomore years are a good time to consider coursework and overall strategy, college planning at this stage should be relatively relaxed. Counselor Sharon F. Drell describes her process this way: "At our school, I do a

FROM THE COUNSELORS

"I like to begin real college search and application work in the fall of the junior year. However, even an 8th grade student could benefit from an introduction to the college search process and goal setting."

—Tracy Spann
Director
Spann College Planning Consultants

College Awareness Night for 9th and 10th graders in about January or February. This is done mainly to calm over-anxious parents and to inform the students and family about what is required in high school (A–G requirements, testing, etc.) in order to apply to college. I ask the 10th and 11th graders early on to take a personality or career assessment to see where their aptitudes lie, and we work from there. Today there are many great online programs to do this."

Junior year?

Though planning early is helpful, the admissions process really gets moving in the junior year. By the 11th grade, students should move forward from taking appropriate course work, focusing on getting good grades, and participating in extra-curricular activities to reading about colleges, visiting campuses, taking required admissions tests, and even beginning the application process. But even so, some students procrastinate, and don't really begin thinking about college in earnest until as late as senior year.

Is it too late to start if I'm a senior?

Independent educational consultant Sue Bigg says, "Senior year is a difficult time to start; [there are] so many 'ughs' about wanting to take easy courses senior year, as well as students dropping foreign language when the requirement has been reached, rushing essays, and teachers who are too busy to write a recommendation for one more student. But remember that there are always colleges with openings into pre-college in August." It might even be a good idea to take some time off and apply to college later. So, whether you still have years ahead of you before college, or if the big move is just around the corner, know that there's always time to consider furthering your education.

"The process should start when the student is ready. Every student has his or her own inner clock. For some, it could start at 14 or 16, for others, at 30. This is very individual. But in general, it is wise to begin serious thinking about college in the spring or summer before junior year."

—William Morse
President
William Morse Associates, Inc.

UNDER THE INFLUENCES

What factors should or shouldn't influence my decision on where to apply?

Archana, senior, Texas, has decent grades and has a college fund in place, so she is looking at private schools and wants to live off campus

There are countless factors to consider when drafting a list of potential colleges to apply to. Often, the factors that seem at first most important to students and parents end up being the least important things in the student's college experience and life after college graduation. The expertise of college counselors can help you to figure out which factors should carry the most weight and which shouldn't really tip the scale in favor of applying to a particular school.

The most common word that counselors use when discussing the college selection process is "fit." Any college can be a dream school for the right student, and any student can find a college that will give him or her a wonderful education and college experience. But the term "fit" encompasses a wide range of other factors. Independent educational consultant Sue Bigg explains what she means by "Goodness of Fit." She says, "This includes teaching style, strengths in student's areas of strength (probably a drawing and painting major wouldn't fare well at an engineering school), distance from home, social fit, size of

FROM THE COUNSELORS

"Look for how you match up to or fit the college. The question often asked in the Common Application Supplement is: 'What attracts you to our college? What makes us a good fit for you?' This is the right approach. Know yourself, and identify your interests, strengths, intellectual and social style, and come up with a list of colleges that fit. Look behind the name and reputation. Find a match."

—William Morse
President
William Morse Associates, Inc.

"I ask each student to create a hypothetical 'perfect college' for himself or herself. Student values and interests sort out beautifully. Money should not limit a student's application list."

—Shirley Bloomquist
Independent college counselor
A Second Opinion

campus and student body, majors in student's high school areas of interest, cost, ease of getting home for holidays, types of graduate schools [alumni have] attended, student relationships with faculty, class size, and college community." Independent counselor Tracy Spann adds more factors, saying that "academic rigor, class size, access to advisors, effectiveness of the career center, location, social and political climate, housing options, strength of curriculum, and internship options should influence a student's decision about applying." We think you'll agree that's quite a lot to consider! But don't worry, there's much more...

The method of balancing these factors is intensely personal. College counselors know how to help you find out which factors will be most important to you. Bill Kellerman, an educational consultant, says, "Students should articulate what they hope to accomplish while at college. They should be able to identify environmental factors that are important to their success." Independent counselor Valerie Broughton says, "The factors that influence each student and family vary according to their own value system. Prestige is very important to some people; it is unimportant to others. I don't decide or judge what's important. I help them decide what factors are important and then find the schools that meet those criteria."

Close to home or far away?
When weighing all these criteria, there are a few that counselors know often end up being very important, and others that will matter less. One thing counselors mention over and over is the importance of being able to easily access and afford travel home. Though many students are eager to make the big leap into the world away from their parents, the frequent trips most students make back to their hometowns for holidays and summer breaks, not to mention for unforeseen family emergencies, can add expenses that financial aid and scholarships

"What should influence your decision: 1) Do I have the educational foundation to be successful here? 2) Do they offer the programs I want to pursue? What should never influence your decision: 1) Money. 2) Is it the largest and most popular school in the state? 3) Did a family member attend?"

—Bruce Richardson
Director of guidance
Plano Sr. High School

"How do you feel being on campus? Do they offer majors, activities, or sports that interest you? Do they have a spiritual focus if that is important to you? Don't worry about the cost as there are many resources to help low income families."

—Rebecca Threewitt
College counselor
The King's Academy

won't cover. And though students may want to get away now, the college experience can become quite difficult if they are the only ones left alone in the dorms over Thanksgiving. This is why counselor, Bruce A. Smith says, "Access to an airport for students who will need to go far away should be considered."

What should not be a factor?
College counselors note three factors that should be of least consideration, but they generally are the very things parents and students are often most worried about: reputation of the college, friends, and cost.

But don't I want a well-known school?
Reputation is often all parents and students have to go on in creating a list of colleges to apply to. However, Farron Peatross, a certified educational planner, says, "Some students, initially, look at schools that they have heard about through sports or relatives, but I urge all students to visit as many schools as possible, because frequently their opinions change after a visit." Certified educational planner Suzanne F. Scott agrees, saying that students "should not be blinded by brand name recognition."

What if my friends are going there?
Additionally, students are often eager to apply to schools because their friends, boyfriends, or girlfriends attend or are planning to attend, but college counselors know this is a big mistake. Bill Kellerman says, "Applying because good friends or the love interest of the moment are applying there is a recipe for disaster." Director of counseling services Carol A. London agrees that "where a parent or friend attended college should not be a factor in deciding upon a college."

But what if cost is my biggest concern?
Though cost of college is a big concern that families should consider, the application stage is the wrong time to consider it. While a college may be expensive, the process of applying for financial aid and scholarships happens alongside the application process, and often schools that look expensive end up being quite affordable when the financial aid packages ring in after the acceptances. Counselor Sharon F. Drell says, "I always advise my students to apply broadly. I encourage private schools even if the family says they cannot afford it. My reasoning is that private schools have larger endowments than public schools that rely on federal and state funds for financial aid. You may receive a financial aid package with fewer loans and more need met from a private school than from a public school. I do make sure students apply to several of each type of college. I never advise them to accept a college offer based only on finances. It must be the right fit, as that is the most important."

LIKE A GLOVE

What exactly does "best fit" mean?

Brad, sophomore, West Virginia, plays football and wants to go to a faith-based school to study sports education

One of the first things any college counselor will tell you is this: Find a college that's a good fit! Well, that sounds great, but what does it mean? Here's what experts have to say about fit and how they advise their students to find it.

First of all, what does it mean to say that schools fit? It means that students will feel comfortable at the schools they choose, both academically and socially. Academically, students will find appropriate majors and courses at the school, and the student will be comfortable with class sizes and the amount of personal attention available from teachers. Socially, students will have the opportunity to find activities that reflect their interests and will feel like they can be themselves, regardless of their politics, beliefs, personal style, race, gender, or sexual orientation. If a school fits, it feels like home.

Consultant Lindy Kahn describes it like this: "The 'best fit' means that a student finds a school that matches their personality (in terms of the social atmosphere), desire for academic rigor and opportunities for service...and the student feels comfortable even if they will be in an area of the country with which they have no experience. There are many more factors too numerous to mention. The 'fit' makes the difference between a happy student and an unhappy one."

How will I know if a school fits?

It's kind of like finding out if an item of clothing fits—you try it on. First of all, it's very important to visit the campus—multiple times, if at all possible. Counselor Leonora Saulino suggests that students visit with professors who teach classes that interest them. Similarly, counselor Margaret Lamb encourages students to spend time doing everyday things on campus. "Visiting the school is probably the most helpful tool students have," she says. "Try out the food! Pick up the campus newspaper, and go when school is in session."

Lamb emphasizes the importance of researching a school as thoroughly as possible by reading promotional materials, looking at the school's website, asking students and professors questions, and visiting campus. She encourages students to become "educated consumers." Lamb asks, "Would you go out to buy a $50,000 car without doing a little background work? College education is a huge investment. It's also a two-way decision: the college decides if it wants you, but equally, you decide if the college is right for you!"

How do I figure out what I'm looking for?

Experts emphasize the importance of figuring out exactly what you're looking for from a school before you start looking. If you're buying an outfit, but you don't know your size or the colors and cuts that look best on you, then you'll have trouble finding the perfect wardrobe. It's like that with a school—if you don't know exactly what you need (or close to it), you'll never find a perfect fit. Counselor Keri Miller explains, "I begin to help a student choose a 'best fit' college by encouraging them to get to know themselves. We talk about goals, both personal and professional. We'll also discuss characteristics they're seeking in a college." Guidance director Mary E. Maloney agrees. "Students need to list their interests, dreams, hobbies, abilities, how they spend their time, grades, strengths, and weaknesses," she explains. "Then search for colleges that match."

FROM THE COUNSELORS

"I use a college and career search engine that asks students excellent questions about what they would like in a college that they may not have thought of in the selection process. For example, it asks how large of a city do they want the school to be set in, what sports do they want the school to participate in, and what size student body is important. One important question that many people don't think about when selecting a college is the climate. I tell students, 'If you don't like cold weather, you might not want to apply to the University of Alaska!'"

—Marie Soderstrom
Senior counselor
Edmond Memorial High School

"I tell students that they are looking for schools where they can be academically successful and socially happy. I give students a list of things to be aware of when visiting a college. When they return from the visit we

Some guidance counselors use an organized system to help students find schools that are a good fit. Counselor Sara Irwin Goudreau explains her system. "I devised a spread sheet. Students, with my help, identify up to 10 schools that they are interested in based on the attributes they have listed on their spread sheet—i.e., major, size of college, location, other interests, study abroad, average freshman GPA, and so forth. They eliminate colleges based on the attributes, or lack thereof. Then I advise them, if possible, to visit the campuses left on the list."

Similarly, counselor Marie Soderstrom relies on a search engine to help students find schools that fit. "I use a college and career search engine that asks students excellent questions about what they would like in a college that they may not have thought of in the selection process," she explains. "For example, it asks how large of a city do they want the school to be set in, what sports do they want the school to participate in, and what size student body is important. One important question that many people don't think about when selecting a college is the climate. I tell students, 'If you don't like cold weather, you might not want to apply to the University of Alaska!'"

There are a lot of factors to take into account, so make sure you start looking at schools in any and every capacity possible. Do lots of research and be sure to visit schools and ask lots of questions. And make sure you know what you want or you'll never know what you're looking for when it comes to the right fit.

discuss what they like about the school and what they don't like about the school. We also look at the course catalogue to make sure that the school offers many classes that sound interesting to the student."

—Marilyn G.S. Emerson
President
College Planning Services, Inc.

"I begin to help a student choose a 'best fit' college by encouraging him to get to know himself. We talk about goals, both personal and professional. We'll also discuss characteristics he is seeking in a college. With this material, we narrow down the list of schools that will provide the student a good fit."

—Keri Miller
Counselor
Minnetonka High School

FROM MAJOR TO CAREER

Is it better to approach college from a career perspective or with the idea that it's supposed to be a growth experience?

Madison, junior, Louisiana, is a cheerleader who is looking for a fun school close to a big city and will probably end up in communications, hopefully something related to TV

Do you know what career you'd eventually like? If not, no worries. Many students exiting high school and entering that exciting first semester in college don't know what career they want. Before you experience a line of work, how can you be expected to know if you'll jump up out of bed excitedly each and every workday for the next 40 years? You can't, and therein lies the dilemma.

This can be a real problem because higher education is so monumentally expensive. You (and your parental units, if they're bankrolling you), don't want to shift gears in educational mid-stream. While you don't absolutely have to be committed to a major/minor and a future profession during the first semester, it's really advantageous to have a general idea which way your career compass needle is pointing.

FROM THE COUNSELORS

"I see college as a place to make one trainable for the job market and/or to provide a background for graduate school. I think students should therefore be in a place where they like the student body and they can get the courses that interest them, but also in an environment that gives them careful teaching, especially in the sciences and in their writing and knowledge of the English language."

–Donald Dunbar
Founder and consultant
Dunbar Educational Consultants, LLC

"Most people change their minds and their majors four or five times in college, as well as their careers later on. I tell students they need to seek out a school that offers a wide enough variety of interests so that they can explore beyond the obvious."

–Deborah Bernstein
Director of college counseling
Forest Ridge School of the Sacred Heart

But the way the system is structured, you do have a little breathing room. How does it work, you ask? It's called the mandatory core curriculum. These are the courses that every student must complete, regardless of major. These generally include literature, English, college algebra, history, and the like. Most institutions also throw in a few of their own favorites.

What if I have no idea what I want to do?

One word: electives. While you're immersed in the joy of the core courses, why not take an elective from the major you're most interested in? Most students find out pretty quickly from taking just one course whether they have chosen wisely. If they haven't, this is the time to bail and choose another major. Much like a police officer, it's always a really good idea to have a backup.

There are also times when, while taking a core course, a student falls head over heels in love with a niche previously not even considered. Another excellent strategy is to spend time talking with fellow students about the course material and other classes they've taken. They're likely to have some strong opinions.

Your counselor's job (part of it, anyway) is to help you find your major. How do they approach it? Debra Holmes-Brown likes to first pose a question to her students: "What do they want to do as a career? What would make them 'happy' if they did this task (job) everyday?" One thing to remember is that your major does not have to be the one that you're best at, the one that comes most easily to you. Nor must it be one that is going to bring you the most money during your working life. Instead, pick the one that you're the most passionate about. Like some man once said, "Do something you love and you'll never work a day in your life."

"I know that students often change their major while in college. However, if a student leans more toward math and science, I will encourage him or her to go to a school with strong math and science programs. If a student's aspirations fall within the liberal arts area, then a student should pick a school that carries a variety of majors within the subject area of interest."

–Deborah C. Curtis
Guidance counselor
Massabesic High School

What if I know exactly what I want to do?

Right, now that you've settled on your major, you've still got those electives to decide on. What to do about that? There are several approaches. One way to look at it, and this is more important in some areas than others, is that you're best served taking classes that focus on your major. Generally speaking, this approach makes the most sense in the more technical majors such as computer science, medicine, physics, or chemistry.

What if I just picked a major because I thought I had to?

A way to get the most out of any major is to pick classes that do not have anything to do with your major. One of the main opportunities in college is to get the broadest education possible. A great number of people find that they end up reinventing themselves several times during their working lives. Take the novelist Michael Crichton, for example. He went all the way through medical school and became a doctor—no small endeavor and certainly no small outlay of greenbacks—but right away he discovered it wasn't for him. So he packed his bags, moved to California, and became a writer. Good for him, sure, but really good for us readers. The thing to get out of this illustration is that Crichton no doubt picked up a knack for writing from some less-technical courses in college, but the in-depth knowledge he acquired from his medical course work became rich fodder for his novels. This was a broad educational experience that paid off in spades.

Is it bad to choose an elective class or a major that is easier for me?

Another approach to selecting electives is to take the easiest courses offered. No, this isn't an idea advanced by an advocacy group for slackers (or perhaps it is). Actually, there are times when this is necessary. Perhaps the courses in your major are so difficult that more of a load would make your career-oriented work suffer. Or perhaps your part-time job has you stretched so thin that more book time is simply impossible. Or maybe you've always wanted to learn how to swing a golf club, and now you can for credit. And it just might be that the classes that come easiest to you are the ones that you love doing. To that end, realize that you can research further into majors that can help you have a career that you love while using the skills that come easiest to you.

No matter what your situation, passion, or talent, you want to put yourself in a winning position early in school. What traits should you develop toward furthering this goal? "Genuine academic interest, personal character, and maturity," is what Donald Dunbar of Dunbar Educational Consultants, LLC advises. Even if the classes seem easy, get serious about your college course work and pay attention to details. Treat your academic progress as a competition not so much with your fellow students, but more yourself—advancement in the working world is competitive, and it starts right where you are: in the high school halls of knowledge.

MARCHING TO THE BEAT OF A DIFFERENT DRUM

What if my intended major is pretty specific?

Jamaal, junior, Colorado, plays music and really wants to go to art school

Maybe you won't need two years of general education classes in college to decide what you want to major in. Maybe you don't need a single college class to tell you what you want to major in because you already know. Maybe you want to be an architect, or a painter, or a guitarist, or a conductor, or even a screenwriter. If so, you'll have a few additional factors to consider as you research schools, not to mention additional steps to take in order to present the most convincing and cohesive portfolio of your talents to the admissions committee.

First, you'll need to consider just how focused a course you want. You could, for example, study music at a liberal arts college that would give you the choice of also earning a teaching credential, or of changing your major, or of doing a double major in another field. You might not, however, have the range of performing opportunities, specialized courses, and individual study that

FROM THE COUNSELORS

"It has to be all about the fit and the program. If it is the right place for the student, meaning program, location, etc., then I say go for it!"

–Sarah Soule
Director of college counseling
Vermont Commons School

"I generally recommend that students choose schools which give them a variety of options in case they decide to change their majors."

–Rachel Elkins Thompson
Director of educational counseling
Douglas L. Thompson, CPA PLLC

you would have at a school that focuses primarily on music. The same is true of other specialized fields. You'll want to read about the choices carefully, talk with people in the field and perhaps current students as well, and also pay close attention to what sort of portfolio, audition, or record of class work, as well as what sort of statement of purpose, the schools you are considering will require of you. And you'll want to include time to prepare these in your application planning.

In many ways this process is similar to choosing a more general course of study. "It has to be all about the fit and the program," says counselor Sarah Soule. "If it is the right place for the student, meaning program, location, etc., then I say go for it!" Mary Kovis Watson is more cautious. "I suggest that students be very careful," she says. Don't get carried away by the idea that going to an art school is going to be just like going to regular college. Keep an eye on your options. "I recommend they look at their local university for an arts education," adds Watson. "It doesn't make sense to pay $100,000 somewhere else for what you could get locally for much, much less." Basically, wanting to go to a specialized college for the sake of simply being there is in the same league as wanting to go to Yale because it's Yale—the best place to go is to the school that is the best fit for your skills and talent.

How do I know if I want a specialized program or school?

It's simple: know what you want. If you choose to enroll in a specialized program, "be sure that you don't want a comprehensive college experience," advises Helene Kunkel. "If you find later that you do, you will have to transfer, and that will change your college experience dramatically." She adds, "Be realistic about job prospects. Even students with MFAs sometimes struggle to find work." Barbara Simmons favors a practical approach to researching your

"Start early. Attend the national fairs and ask for a preliminary review of your portfolio."

–Kate McVey
Director of college advising
Brebeuf Jesuit Preparatory School

options. "I always tell our students to look at what the alumni of such schools are now doing, to look at what courses the specific department the student's interested in offers, and to look at the faculty vitae to see how active the faculty is," she says.

"I generally recommend that students choose schools which give them a variety of options in case they decide to change their majors," says Rachel Elkins Thompson. "However, if I have a student whose only interest is fashion or art or the like, I help him or her find the right program." There are many different fields and sorts of work within a specialization, as well as many different ways to train for them. Think about the different ways you could approach your interests. Are there particular areas within an interest that you would like to explore? What kind of options would you have to use your interests after graduation? By thinking about this before even getting to college, you'll be able to have a clear idea of what you want and how you can get it, not to mention whether or not you may change your mind about what you want to study, which could impact how happy you are at the school you decide to enroll at. This can be a stressful issue, but keep in mind that many—if not all—students question whether they really want to study what they're studying. Many will change their majors several times before finding the right one. Ronna Morrison has a tip on how to avoid any surprises: "Try a summer program after junior year to test the depth of your interest." Once you know your direction, "start early [on getting feedback]," advises Kate McVey. "Attend the national fairs and ask for a preliminary review of your portfolio."

Deep down, you know whether or not you want to pursue something. With art, as with all things in life, passion and perseverance will determine your success, so if you truly want to enroll in a specialized program or college, go for it! If you're unsure, there's no harm starting at a larger university and then transferring later on (or not) when you've got a clearer idea of what you want. "I advise students to be very sure they want a specialized curriculum," says Renee L. Goldberg. "I have seen many students who transfer from art or music or other specialized colleges because they want a broader education. I encourage them to visit a few specialized colleges as well [to see if the campus scene seems like a good fit.]"

TRUTH IN ADVERTISING?

How important is reputation or name recognition when it comes to choosing a college?

Mark, junior, North Carolina, is an A-student who wants to go to an Ivy League school

Ever spend $100 on a pair of jeans simply because of the designer label? Fair enough, lots of high school students do that. But have you ever spent $160,000 on a college education because of a designer label? Maybe not yet, but that doesn't mean it couldn't happen. The question is, as good as that school will look on your résumé, is it worth the price tag? What if you have the money (or the financial aid), along with a big fat admissions packet to a prestigious school? Is it worth it to attend? How important should name recognition of reputation be when you're selecting a college?

While everyone can agree that the names Harvard, Columbia, and Princeton immediately conjure up ideas of academic greatness, very few of the counselors we spoke to agree that you should let a school's name influence your decision to attend. In fact, even the independent counselors in this survey, who work with many students and families who are hoping for big-name school results, agree. For example, admissions consultant Lloyd R. Paradiso has a handy answer when it comes to how much name recognition should matter. "Zero," he says. "What does it mean? Who really knows what Hamilton or Carleton or even Yale is, for that matter? Precious few."

So, what really matters?

Most experts argue that what really matters is fit. You need to find schools that give you the opportunity to study what you want while matching your personality and learning style and preparing you for the working world. "Name and reputation do little for you when you actually select a college," argues counselor Keri Miller. "They offer little more than the 'ahhh' factor you receive from others when you tell them what school you will be attending. The name and reputation of a school do not necessarily mean it is the best college for you, your goals, your abilities, and your personality." Consultant Marilyn

G.S. Emerson agrees. "To me, the most important criteria when choosing a college is the fit," says Emerson. "For some students and families, the school's name or reputation is very important initially, but it becomes less so as they learn more about the large number of colleges and universities across the country." Counselor Lisa Post adds that when students focus on choosing a brand name college instead of fit, they lose out. "For our students, name recognition is very important, which means they sometimes miss out on a gem of a school because it does not have the Ivy label," says Post.

Other experts argue that it's not the name of the school that matters, but what the student can accomplish at that school. Look at it this way: anyone can blow $160,000 on a college education and end up with a fancy name on their diploma, but it's those students who take full advantage of every academic and social opportunity their college offers who come out ahead. "I personally think that college is what you make of it," says consultant Rachel Winston. "Great schools can be tormenting or frustrating to some while engaging and exciting to others." Consultant Marilyn Morrison agrees. "Students should look past brand names when selecting a college," says Morrison. "It's less about where they go to college and much more about what they do when they get there."

Ultimately, all college dreams are subject to financial concerns. "Younger students go strictly on name recognition," says counselor Marie Soderstrom. "However, as the reality of paying for college sets in, scholarships or financial packets become very important to the majority of students."

FROM THE COUNSELORS

"To me, the most important criteria when choosing a college is the fit. For some students and families, the school's name or reputation is very important initially, but becomes less so as they learn more about the large number of colleges and universities across the country."

—Marilyn G.S. Emerson
President
College Planning Services, Inc.

What if I want to go to graduate school?

Another school of thought is that name recognition is important—but only when choosing a graduate or professional school. The right name on a job application can make a difference in careers such as law, business, or academia, but this is much less likely to be a factor for a student earning an undergraduate degree. As consultant Lindy Kahn explains, "Reputation or name recognition comes into play more when going for a post-secondary degree (i.e., law or med school). What you achieve as an undergraduate should outweigh the school's public reputation."

So are designer schools worth it? Experts agree that those names are worth something and will certainly look impressive as you look for jobs or apply to grad schools. But almost everyone in this survey feels that the value of big name schools is overstated and that students are better off looking for the school that fits best than the one with the designer name. As a matter of fact, it's not so different from a pair of jeans at all.

"Name and reputation are popular characteristics for students researching colleges. However, name and reputation do little for you when you actually select a college. They offer little more than the 'ahhh' factor you receive from others when you tell them what school you will be attending. The name and reputation of a school do not necessarily mean it is the best college for you, your goals, your abilities, and your personality."

—Keri Miller
School counselor
Minnetonka High School

MO' MONEY, MO' PROBLEMS?

Should I apply to a school I can't afford?

Pratik, freshman, New Jersey, is a track star and wants to get an athletic scholarship because his grades are not that strong

Money is a major concern for many families when they first begin creating a list of possible colleges and universities to which their student might apply. But the question of whether or not students should apply to schools they know they can't afford contains an inherent assumption: that they can know whether or not they can afford a school before applying there.

The fact is that a school's sticker price is the actual out-of-pocket expense for only a few families. Most students receive some sort of financial aid, whether it comes in the form of merit scholarships, need-based aid, grants, loans, work-study programs, or fee waivers. And the full picture of how much aid a student will receive to cover the cost of attendance does not emerge until after the application process.

For this reason, most college counselors recommend that students apply to all the schools that are a good academic, social, and personal fit for them and aggressively seek all financial aid options available to them from the very beginning. Even wealthy families should at least fill out the Free Application for Federal Student Aid (FAFSA), so that they know what options are available to them.

Valerie Broughton, an independent counselor, explains it this way: "Students don't know if they can afford a school or not until all of the scholarship and financial aid awards are announced. I explain to families that regardless of their financial situation, the value question, 'Is this college worth the money?' is always an issue. So, my students apply to the colleges where there's a good fit, including some less expensive colleges that meet their criteria. The time to consider the net cost is after all of the information is available. We consider it at the end of the process, not so much at the beginning." Independent counselor Trey Chappell agrees. He says, "You really don't know if you can afford it until your award letters come in. Applying keeps your options open."

Of course, it's important to keep less expensive options open as well. Not only should students apply to expensive schools and hope for financial aid but, also, they should consider some less expensive alternatives. When money is a major factor, counselors agree that it is important to apply to some schools that are more affordable. Director of guidance Scott White says, "You never know what financial aid you'll get...but make sure you have a financial safety school." Independent educational consultant Sue Bigg agrees. She says, "Financial aid can make the most needy student able to attend, but a financial range should be in the application mix."

But what if I think I'll get a lot of scholarship money?

You can't count on getting a full ride. Students should apply to some schools that they would love to attend even though they'll be a financial reach, but you should definitely apply to some financial safety schools in case the financial aid award doesn't cover enough of the cost of attendance at the expensive schools. Bill Kellerman, an educational consultant, explains, "Students should be realistic about their options. Colleges may not offer them the aid they need to attend. Complete the FAFSA and the Profile. Remain hopeful. Consider opportunities to earn money while attending college. Consider taking a gap year or semester to earn the money. Apply for the outside scholarships and grants you are eligible for. Create a realistic plan of action, then ask the college if it is doable."

Can't I just get my own loans to pay for school?

It's essential to keep in mind that financial aid for college is related to the entire family's income. Though a student may be willing to take on student loans to attend an expensive school, the federal government always considers the Expected Family Contribution (EFC) in offering those loans. Occasionally, parents are unwilling to share their financial information on the FAFSA, or they are unwilling or unable to make the EFC to their student's education. Independent counselor Shirley Bloomquist notes that "parents should level with students about finances." Co-director of college counseling Letitia W. Peterson says, "[Students] should apply to expensive schools only if they and their parents are willing to do the work to complete the paperwork for need-based aid. Those colleges should be balanced with others that are affordable."

Though many students and their parents may think that certain colleges are out of their reach, they should know that anything is possible if the family gets an early start on applying for financial aid. Counselor Scott Fisch says, "The only thing they are risking is the application fee. I think it can be a really positive thing for a student to be accepted to a 'dream school' even though he may not be able to afford it up front."

FROM THE COUNSELORS

"Financial aid is so varied, and it costs very little to apply versus to attend, so why not leave that door open?"

—Trey Chappell
Director
College X-ing, LLC

"Financial need is relative, depending on the total cost of attendance at each school, so I encourage students to apply to colleges regardless of the cost. Just as they are encouraged to have a range of colleges based on selectivity, I recommend that students include a couple of colleges, which without financial aid, would be out of reach."

—Tracy Spann
Director
Spann College Planning Consultants

IVY OR BUST

What can an Ivy League school do for me?

Ashley, senior, Tennessee, volunteers her time with non-profits and is considering a 5-year bachelor's/master's program

When it comes to the Ivies, guidance counselors and experts are in strong agreement. No, Ivy League graduates do not lead more successful lives. And yes, there are many scenarios in which a student should turn down an offer of admission to an Ivy League school.

First of all, experts claim that there is no evidence that Ivy League graduates are more successful than graduates of non-Ivy colleges. "There are plenty of studies to show that going to an Ivy League school is not a predictor or guarantee of success," says educational consultant Jody Zodda. "I always hand my students a list of famous people who went to colleges you never heard of on the day I give them their college lists." College counselor Katie Small agrees: "Some Ivy Leaguers are spectacularly successful. Then again, so are many community college graduates."

"Ivy League graduates are not superhuman. Some Ivy Leaguers are spectacularly successful; then again, so are many community college graduates. In the long run, successful lives are made by determined individuals, regardless of pedigree."

–Katie Small
College counselor
The Princeton Review

"Ivy League graduates are not necessarily more successful than graduates from other schools.

At the end of the day, while [attending an Ivy] may get you a leg up on your first job, it is how you perform on the job that determines your success. There are plenty of studies to show that going to an Ivy League school is not a predictor or guarantee of success. I always hand my students a list of famous people who went to colleges you never heard of on the day I give them their college list."

–Judy Zodda
Educational consultant
Zodda College Services

If an Ivy isn't the key to success, what is?

While experts agree that an Ivy League background can provide tangible advantages in the working world, they argue that these are not nearly as important as the willingness to work hard. As educational planner Judi Robinovitz argues, "An Ivy League college will certainly open doors, but it's then up to the graduate to achieve success after he or she walks through those doors." Katie Small agrees. "In the long run," she says, "successful lives are made by determined individuals, regardless of pedigree."

Other experts question what the meaning of "success" should be—and whether it can be the defined by the financial advantages that sometimes come from having an Ivy League education. "Of course, Ivy League grads are not more successful," says college counseling director Jon Reider. "What is success? Money, happiness, high status? Freud said the most successful lives have 'love and work.' What college can provide that?" Reider adds that his own two children attended Ivy League schools and he doesn't feel that there's anything wrong with going to them—just that "they aren't as special as people think." He adds, "What makes these the best schools besides snobbery?"

Why would I turn down an Ivy League school?

So, under what circumstances should a student turn down admission to an Ivy League school? Experts strongly emphasize that when it comes to choosing a school, overall fit is far more important than Ivy League status. "Students should seek the college that best matches them," says Katie Small. "The best school is not always the most difficult school that accepts them. If a student does not want to live in the library, then he or she should not attend Stanford or Dartmouth. If a student wants to excel and stand out, then he should not pit himself against the biggest fish he can find." Educational consultant Jon W. Tarrant agrees: "It's all about fit or match. Students should attend colleges they love, not necessarily ones with the most bumper sticker appeal at the country club."

College counselor Jennifer DesMaisons feels especially strongly about the importance of fit because she herself once attended an Ivy League school that was a poor fit, and she eventually transferred out as a junior. "There are absolutely times when a student should turn down admission to an Ivy League school," says DesMaisons, "such as when and if a student discovers that another school could better help him or her achieve their personal and academic goals."

Of course, as with any other question of fit, experts argue that Ivy League schools are a better fit for some students than others. For example, if a student is searching for a specific major that's hard to find, an Ivy League school might be the best fit if that major is offered—and it might not be the best fit if that major is not offered. Other considerations are important as well. Consultant June Wang Scortino argues, "I strongly believe the Ivy schools are not suitable for many first-generation college students."

One reason that students may turn down acceptance to an Ivy League school is obvious—money. Experts strongly urge students to consider the financial implications of an Ivy League education, as the astronomical prices often just aren't worth it. "If a student's matriculation at an Ivy League school will cause undue financial hardship to a family, then the student should not enroll," says counseling director Lester Eggleston, Jr. "It takes away from their overall college experience."

Experts do not dispute the fact that an Ivy League education can lead to the economic advantages that come with the ability to put an Ivy League name on your résumé, as well as the power of networking. However, all things considered, most experts feel that the benefits of attending an Ivy League school have been wildly overstated. Other issues, such as fit and affordability, are valued much more highly.

FACING FACTS

Why do people keep telling me that going to an Ivy League school is unrealistic?

Katie, senior, Delaware, has lots of AP credits and is the school's valedictorian, and she wants to go to grad school

Students often dream big. Setting sights high and working hard to achieve goals are great aspirations for young people about to embark on the adventure of adulthood. However, in a media market saturated by the reputation of a few big-name colleges and universities, students can end up aspiring to schools that probably won't admit the student, and that are poor choices as far as the needs of the student. For this reason, counselors often find themselves in the position of explaining to students that though they may not be admitted to the school whose initials they see emblazoned on sweatshirts everywhere, they may still be able to find an excellent match for them, personally. Independent counselor Tracy Spann says that when she begins to work with a family, "Every student receives a tutorial in evaluating a solid academic fit. Once the academic fit has been determined, it is important for students to be able to identify the characteristics that will make a college a good social and personal match."

FROM THE COUNSELORS

"I have a strict safety school, reality school, and dream (reach) school policy. Students should have a bare minimum of one of each and a maximum of eight total. If they have more than that, they haven't really done their research. I don't think it's possible to have dozens of schools that are going to be a good fit."

–Ellen E. Underwood
Lead counselor
R.L. Turner High School

"I use statistics and odds. Although not exact, I like to estimate students' chances at the colleges one by one, based on recent data. They have to know that nothing is guaranteed until they step foot in that college classroom on day one."

–Trey Chappell
Director
College X-ing, LLC

Other counselors agree that the competitiveness of the admissions system often causes students to focus too much on whether they can get in somewhere rather than whether they should attend that college or university. To help students to avoid this misstep, independent counselor Sandra Bramwell-Riley says that counselors should "give a cross-section of schools from the get-go!" Counselor Teresa Knirck tells her students, "There is a place for everyone; just find it."

Remember, too, that it isn't just about what the school can do for you, but what you can do for the school. Counselor Sheila Nussbaum says "I want to see students have a balanced list with a range of cost and competitiveness on their list. I make sure there are schools on their list that value their presence on their campus."

What's the best way to define "realistic"?

While matching a student with a college that is likely to be a good academic, personal, and social fit is the great art of the college admissions counselor, predicting whether or not a student will get into a particular school is more of a science. Though there are always happy surprises, and most counselors strongly advise that students apply to dream schools that are "reaches," the number one predictor of college admissions is still the numbers. When students are overly focused only on schools that are highly competitive, counselor Bruce A. Smith says, "Objective data such as found in the common data set, school website and publications, and guides such as The Princeton Review (and others) helps put things in perspective."

"I want students to dream. But they must then back up dreams with commitment. Vision is essential, but it must be backed up by all-consuming passion, discipline, and drive."

–William Morse
President
William Morse Associates, Inc.

This databased perspective is something many counselors try to instill in their students. Letitia W. Peterson, a co-director of college counseling, says "We use data from previous applicants from our school to help students get a general sense of their chances of admission." For counselors, being sensitive to the hopes of families is important, but statistics can help to provide knowledge that may temper high expectations with a dose of realism. Certified educational planner Suzanne F. Scott likes to "use objective data to empower student and family to arrive at realistic conclusions, through ongoing dialogues." Similarly, certified educational planner Susan Hanflik says, "I am reality-based and pull no punches. I use prior admission criteria to educate families, and offer alternatives that are appropriate."

And if my parents still insist on the Ivies?

Even when counselors work hard to build realistic expectations, there are still some students and parents who insist that they are only interested in the most competitive colleges, especially the Ivy League. Independent educational consultant Sue Bigg has particular words for these students. She tells them, "You're well qualified for Ivy Heaven, but so are 90 percent of their applicant pool, and they turn down 90 percent of applicants. Here are some other fine colleges that are 'likelies' and will allow me to sleep at night. I'd rather have a few happy surprises than a stash of thin envelopes." She adds, "I tell students that 'reaches' are easy to find, and I'm going to help them find great 'likelies.'" Counselor Sharon F. Drell agrees, noting, "For students applying to Ivy League schools, I am constantly saying how tough it is to gain admission to these schools. [The schools] have not expanded their admissions numbers, but there are thousands more who apply. I explain that students need to apply very broadly, and to other types of schools. You certainly cannot count on admission [to Ivies], even if you have straight A's and a 2400 SAT. You need to stand out in some other way: sports, community service, etc." Educational Consultant Suzanne Luce puts it a little more bluntly: "I bring out the tissue box, then I show the résumés of some of my students attending Ivy League colleges."

No matter what type of school you are interested in attending, it is important both to reach high and to acknowledge the possibilities of schools that might not have been your top choice. As Shirley Bloomquist, an independent college counselor, says, "I support student dreams while showing them data on acceptances. I encourage students and parents to keenly attend to 'likely' schools."

A PENNY SAVED IS A PENNY LEARNED

I got accepted into my first-choice school, but I can't afford it. What are my options?

Ahmed, junior, Iowa, is a gamer who is considering pre-law

Congratulations! You've been accepted by your first choice school! It is unfortunate, however, that you don't think you can swing the tuition and that what the college offers to offset the cost isn't enough to make it work.

There are several routes to go. First off, before you even applied to schools you should have done your research to make sure that you could afford them. "I try to make sure students have a financial safety school," says Barbara Bayley. Even if you didn't think about this beforehand, now might be the time to look at your options with a money-based perspective.

What if I really want to go to that first-choice school?

Remember to take a step back so you can fully assess the situation. "Discuss the differences and attributes for your first and second choice schools, as well as the difference in cost," says Bruce Barrett. It's not just about the next four years, either. "Take a look at what this will mean to you in the long haul," says Ann Harris. "Compare your offers. Is there now a compelling reason to go to a different school? Are you thinking about pursuing a career that will require grad school?" If you have an eye on a master's or doctorate after undergrad, keep in mind that you'll need some money left to pay for that. According to Angela Conley, one way of saving money is by exploring "transfer programs that may make attendance amenable at a later point."

"I advise students to write a letter appealing to the financial aid office for further funds," says Andrea Badger. "Let them know you really want to go to school there." While you're doing this, she also advises that you "search out scholarships, in particular local ones based in your community." There might be resources from local and regional civic groups, religious organizations, or even businesses in a particular field of study. Counselors and librarians can be excellent resources for tracking down these elusive—but often lucrative—ways to build you college war chest. Nancy W. Cadwallader says, "First, students should see that all funds at the school are exhausted (i.e., work study, jobs on campus, etc.). If so, then they should project costs and determine if they can handle a loan. If they don't think they can, they should choose another school." There are plenty of places out there happy to give college loans—banks, credit unions, specialized companies—but be honest with yourself about your financial situation. If you don't think you'll be able to meet those monthly payments, it's probably best to take a pass and put your cash toward a more financially feasible educational experience.

You might also consider part-time attendance or distance learning courses so that you can work while studying. Another option is to ask for deferred admission so you can work full-time and save money, knowing that you'll have a spot at the school next year.

"Going into it, it is really important for students who will be dependent upon financial aid to approach this situation with an open mind," says Christine Assmussen. "Some things just do not work out in life, but if you have lined up a range of good options, you will be fine." Barbara Pasalis adds, "Students always need to know that there is not only one right college for them—many colleges can be right for a student." There are plenty of great fits out there for you—and oftentimes the best fit will be the school (not to sound too much like a commercial) that combines the academics you want with the price tag you require. If all else fails, remember that colleges want to gain students, not

FROM THE COUNSELORS

"Going into it, it is really important for students who will be dependent upon financial aid to approach this situation with an open mind...if you have lined up a range of good options, you will be fine."

–Christine Asmussen
Director of college counseling
St. Andrew's—Sewanee School

"I encourage students and parents to talk to someone in the financial aid office, and I also encourage them to not be afraid to accept college loans."

–Alicia Curry
Counselor
Juan Seguin High School

lose them, meaning that you might have more leverage than you think when it comes to negotiating financial aid. Follow Ann Montgomery's advice and "call the financial aid office and discuss it—they want to help." And as independent counselor Jill Madenberg says, "Plenty of expensive schools have plenty of money to give."

"Take a look at what this will mean to you in the long haul."

—Ann Harris
Director of college guidance
Parish Episcopal School

FINANCIALLY SOUND

Is there a way to make the financial aid process any easier?

Philip, senior, Washington, hasn't taken standardized tests and is thinking of going to community college and transferring

The financial aid process is complicated and confusing—but is it the role of a college counselor to walk students and parents through the process? Experts have very different opinions about this issue. Some guidance counselors and educational consultants do little or nothing to help with the financial aid process and do not see this as a part of their job. However, according to the experts we surveyed, most are willing to help students and parents through their process.

Some counselors and consultants do very little to help families with financial aid, but don't take it personally—after all, they're college counselors, not financial counselors. "I tell them to fill out the financial aid application," says counselor Kathy McCasland. Consultant Marilyn G.S. Emerson does the same, but goes one step further—she tells parents to go talk to their accountants. Consultant Lindy Kahn explains, "Typically, I do not counsel parents on

FROM THE COUNSELORS

"I sit down with any parents who are interested in financial aid and walk them step-by-step through the process. If they like, I will have them fill out the FAFSA and CSS Profile in my office and discuss what is required in each of the blanks."

–Rachel Winston
President
College Counseling Center

"Funding is one of the most ignored factors in college admissions counseling because most counselors, school and independent alike, don't understand it...I will work with my clients unless their situation is too complex and beyond my ability to assist, at which point I will recommend trusted colleagues."

–Lloyd R. Paradiso
President and CEO
The Admissions Authority

financial aid, other than to suggest colleges that are more likely to grant merit aid based on their child's record." Other counselors refer students to websites for assistance.

However, most counselors are more hands-on when it comes to financial aid. One common thing that schools do is to bring in expert speakers for families—especially because counselors themselves can feel pretty confused by the complex process. "We hold a financial aid night presented by a representative of the Massachusetts Financing Authority," says counselor Leslie R. Munn. Counselor Margaret Lamb says, "We provide a financial aid presentation to the parents of 9th graders—and 10th graders, if they missed it the year before. It is presented by a speaker from the Northeastern University Financial Aid Office. He gives a great overview of what to expect—an early head's up. During junior year, we do another presentation for parents that includes financial aid information, and in senior year there is a financial aid presentation done by another local college."

Another thing that some schools do to help families is to offer them financial aid literature. While some schools create their own forms, others copy information from experts and agencies. "Great handouts are available from lending institutions," says counselor Marie Soderstrom. It's also common for schools to create websites to convey information to families about deadlines, forms, and other important information. In addition, many schools offer parent financial aid nights in order to distribute information and answer questions.

"We offer financial aid nights for parents to attend," says counselor Keri Miller. "In addition, we offer printed materials in the Counseling Office for parent support. Finally, if needed, parents meet with us individually. I also recommend that parents contact the financial aid office of their child's prospective

"We keep an active website for parents. We have parent programs in the evening, and we offer FAFSA assistance in the evening."

–Leonora Saulino
Guidance counselor
Taunton High School

college." Needless to say, if your high school hosts anything along these lines, it'd behoove you to partake and to let your parents know.

Some counselors and schools are even more active in giving financial aid help, and in some cases are willing to offer parents direct assistance with the FAFSA and other important paperwork. "Since almost all of my students will be first-generation college students, I have to do a lot of handholding through the FAFSA," says counselor Lynda McGee. Consultant Rachel Winston does the same. "I sit down with any parents who are interested in financial aid and walk them step-by-step through the process," she explains. "If they like, I have them fill out the FAFSA and CSS Profile in my office and discuss what is required in each of the blanks."

Counselor Marie Soderstrom's school is especially helpful with financial aid. "The first thing I do is send home a letter to senior parents regarding the financial aid process," explains Soderstrom. "I encourage them to order their pin numbers immediately so they don't get caught in the rush in January of the senior year. I then meet with every senior in small groups and go over the process, and then send handouts home for their parents. I explain in detail the different types of aid because most students and parents aren't aware of the different types of aid available. It is the parents who really care about this information, so I try to give them as much information as possible."

So how involved should your counselor be in the financial aid process? Well, it's up to them, really. But if you need help, they're there for you, and don't forget checking out other options as well. As with most things in life, if you need some illumination when it comes to financial aid, all you have to do is ask.

RESIDENCY RULES

Is it better to apply to a state school as an out-of-state resident or to pick a private college?

Brady, 8th grader, Arizona, home-schooled, wants to go far from home

Counselors frequently advise that the best value for a college education is usually an in-state public school. Most states have excellent universities at affordable prices. However, you may not find a good fit at one of your state colleges. Perhaps all the public schools are very big, and you are looking for something a bit more intimate, or maybe none of the state schools offer the major you are most interested in. Furthermore, if you are an international student or you have moved recently and don't meet the residency requirements to apply to public schools at the in-state tuition rates, then you might have to research other options.

Some counselors believe that applying to out-of-state public colleges and universities is not as good an option, financially, as applying to a private school. Independent counselor Valerie Broughton explains: "It is very rare that I put an out-of-state [public] school on a student's list. The cost of out-of-state tuition can't usually be justified. Of course, if the out-of-state public university has a particular program that the in-state university does not, the out-of-state choice may be more appropriate. But because out-of-state universities rarely offer much scholarship money, the cost of out-of-state universities may be more than a private school's, where the student may qualify for merit aid. I've found that the very selective state schools—such as UVA, UCLA, UNC, and Penn State, for example—have become very selective for out-of-state students. That's another reason they don't show up on most of my students' lists." Independent counselor Tracy Spann agrees, explaining that "many states cap the number of students they can admit from out-of-state, making admission more selective. They may not have as much scholarship money to devote to out-of-state students as a private school would have, since there is no distinction between in- or out-of-state."

However, counselor Sharon F. Drell has a different perspective. She says, "Some out-of-state colleges relish out-of-staters and actually entice them with some large financial aid offers...You must remember if you are from out-of-state, most likely your friends will not be from your hometown. My daughter went to the University of Michigan and made friends all up and down the East Coast and in the Midwest." Director of guidance Scott White also mentions that there are some state schools, "like U. Mass., that are looking for out-of-state students."

Nearly all counselors agree that funding can be easier to get from private colleges. Educational consultant Sue Bigg mentions that though "the in-state public college is usually the least expensive option, a private college may cost less by virtue of dispersing excellent merit scholarships." Counselor Sheila Nussbaum agrees that private colleges "might offer more merit money for a strong student."

Are there options other than financial differences?

On the surface, weighing the option of applying to a public school out-of-state versus applying to a private college is primarily a question of finances. But often, the financial difference between these two alternatives is small. Counselor Bruce A. Smith acknowledges that "if the college is a good fit, and the finances are similar, I don't think it makes a difference." And even in situations where there is a difference in the cost, there are other factors to consider. Suzanne F. Scott, a certified educational planner, says, "The important thing is to carefully evaluate a student's prospects and goodness of fit with his or her goals, and select a broad list of schools where he or she has realistic prospects that can, of course, include some reaches." Educational consultant Bill Kellerman echoes this sentiment. He says, "Applying to the colleges that best meet

FROM THE COUNSELORS

"I think there are a number of large out of state public universities that are worth the tuition and the expense. I also think that a number of private schools do a great job at providing the full college experience, while some private schools could be a waste of money for some students."

—Trey Chappell
Director
College X-ing, LLC

the student's needs and provide the most opportunities to accomplish the student's goals is the best option."

Remember that since financial aid decisions come after admissions decisions, most students don't know the actual cost of the schools they apply to until the very end of the process. This means that applying to all the schools that would match a student's personal and educational goals, whether the college is in-state, out-of-state, or a private school, is a good idea.

"There is no 'better option' for every student. It depends on what is a good fit for the individual."

—Letitia W. Peterson
Co-director of college counseling
Holton-Arms School

FIRST IN LINE

What should I keep in mind as a first-generation student?

Trang, senior, New York, doesn't speak fluent English and is looking for a large-school experience

Being the first in your family to go to college can seem overwhelming, for you and your family. Any guidance counselor will tell you that it's best to have your parents as closely involved in the search process as possible. According to Farron Peatross, a certified education planner, too often "families underestimate the living and personal expenses [of the college experience]." For this reason, don't be surprised if your counselor treats you and your parents as one in the same (as if you're both going to college), because although "some of the parents' questions and concerns may seem basic to those of us with experience, their sincere interest in helping their children further their education is great," says Valerie Broughton, president of College Connectors.

FROM THE COUNSELORS

"You are not alone. Even students with college-educated parents and siblings have the same fears."

–Bill Kellerman
Educational consultant
College 101

"Any student can go to college if the motivation is there."

–Teresa Knirck
Guidance counselor
Hanford High School

Do I really have to talk to my parents and counselor so much about finding the right college?

Feel free to do your own research and to make some decisions, but your parents and counselors are an important part of the entire college admissions process. It's possible the search process will test the mettle and patience of your counselor and your parents as much as it does yours, and communication is important. Sue Bigg, an educational consultant, leaves no stone unturned. "Talk at great length about college, what it's like and what its benefits are." Bigg is fond of taking students and their parents on a tour of a local college, "pointing out factors they should look at." Also, communicate with the students on campus and try to find other first-generation students who are going through the same experience that you are.

If it ever seems like your counselor and parents are talking to you like you're an 8-year-old, cut them some slack. They're trying to make doubly sure you understand what's at stake. The language is never more cut and dry than when the conversation turns to money—as in, financial aid. Good guidance will introduce you to the wonders of need-based scholarships, as well as merit-based ones. Applications for FAFSA will require a lot of time and patience, and they will have to be gone through line by line, in order to construe how large a subsidized loan you can expect. More than any other aspect of the college search, the money talk will be a strenuous exercise in communication. And though it will be frustrating, don't give up and keep in mind that you should be proud of your accomplishment.

Independent counselor Jill Madenberg stresses the importance of making sure that you, a first-generation college student-to-be, "identify yourself as such." It's an important identity to acknowledge, not because you should

"You have no idea what adventures and eye-opening experiences you will enjoy at college. I also explain how many scholarships are available for first-generation students. If you are really high-achieving, you will barely have to pay for much of your college expenses."

–Sharon F. Drell
College counselor
Grover Cleveland High School

wear it like a scarlet letter, but because as you go through the semesters at your chosen college, any number of things will come up—administrative issues like loan renewals—that you will need to know how to anticipate and take care of. So listen closely from the very start and keep all your paperwork in order. Your folks at home, after all, will be counting on you.

BEYOND THE SEA

What do I do if I want to study abroad?

Stacey, freshman, Oregon, has good standardized tests but a so-so GPA and lots of extracurriculars, and she is thinking of taking a year off to study in Europe

So you went to Paris last summer with the family, and one sultry night after the parents finally turned in, you tiptoed down to the hotel lobby to meet Philippe—bellboy by day, bohemian poet by night—as he ended his shift, whereupon he offered you a Gitane (a French cigarette, because you're old enough there) before lifting you onto his scooter to go whizzing through the cobbled streets and along the Seine till sunrise scaled the girders of the Eiffel Tower—sigh, the time to kiss, bid adieu and go back, secretly. But not before exchanging e-mails.

When the promise of freedom and independence after high school graduation isn't enough in the American context, fantasies like this one take flight. Just admit, though, that it never happened. Besides, Mom and Dad have made it clear that while a semester or two abroad is one thing, four whole years outside the country is out of the question—unless you can make a good case, and it had better be your best one yet. Most college counselors will need to be convinced, too, especially given the unmatched quality and range of academic options available to American students within their own country. Nevertheless, if it's anywhere but here that you want to be, you have a lot to consider. Counselor Jane Mathias puts the onus on you to "do extensive research and understand the implications of being that far from home." Ask yourself some important questions. Do I speak the language there? How well do I know the culture? Do the course credits and degree programs at the university compare favorably to those in the United States? And with a foreign diploma, can I get a job when I come home?

Jennifer Tabbush, president of Headed for College, says that, after the language barrier question is answered, "the process [of searching for the right school] is identical" to that of looking within the United States, "in that we are looking for a match across academics, culture of the school, campus community, professors, opportunities, etc." To sidestep worries that your degree from abroad won't stack up stateside, counselor Diana Hedstrom advises you "to check into colleges in the United States that offer exchange programs abroad," because these colleges will ensure that your degree is more or less a U.S. equivalent.

Ultimately, don't be surprised if you're the only one who supports your dream of study sessions in a Montmartre café. With the exception of Canada and, by English-speaking extension, the UK and Australia, your guidance counselor probably isn't going to volunteer many suggestions. The right decision for you may come out of listening to trustworthy people around you: your parents, your teachers (especially your language instructor) and counselors, foreign exchange students in your high school, and, above all, yourself. Once you're past allowing a semester abroad as an option, when "anywhere else but here" is not a novelty but something you firmly believe will guide you into a vibrant and successful adulthood, then you should probably start applying for your passport, so get those photos taken and don't forget to smile.

FROM THE COUNSELORS

"A reality check is the first factor [in picking a college abroad]! The best institution is the one that is possible to attend. Many criteria are reviewed in this analysis—academic performance and finances being the first two."

–Rosa Moreno
College counselor
Caracas Private School District

"Thoroughly research your choice, be in contact with that country's consulate, and speak with students who attended the college."

–Hazel M. Shaw
College guidance counselor
James Madison High School

A DAY AT THE FAIR

Will a college fair really help me pick a college?

Steve, senior, Massachusetts, worked really hard for average GPA and standardized test scores despite a learning disability, and he wants to live in a dorm and study nursing

When the college fair comes to your high school cafeteria, make a point to go. What you're going to find are a configuration of tabletops shingled in glossy tri-fold brochures, complimentary logoed pens and keychains, and, of course, the chirpy, toothy (and oft blue-blazered) recruiters who would love more than anything to have a word with you about the "campus experience" they have to offer you. Don't be afraid of these people. They are genuinely kind and interested in you—which is why they do this for a living. Just be aware of a few things: Every school claims to be the "Harvard of (general U.S. region)" and anyone you give your e-mail address to will be in touch.

A snapshot of one of these college fairs may be what the inside of your head might look like right now—busy, confusing, and (at times) overwhelming. With so many schools pulling your heart in so many directions, the schools and the promises the recruiters make can all start to blur together. Therefore it's vital, says counselor Hazel M. Shaw, that you "make the effort to remain organized"

"I recommend many resources, including view books, college websites, search websites, and visit if at all possible. Be organized, keep notes, and investigate the academic, social, and financial fit of a school for you (not your friends, not your parents). Continue contact with the school so that when it comes time to make a decision, you have as much information as you need to make a good one."

—Jane Mathias
Director of guidance
Nardin Academy

"Start early! My most successful clients have begun in the 7th grade."

—Janice M. Hobart
CEO
College Found

during your search. "If not, this adds to the stress." Whether you're dog-ear-ing pages in **The Best 371 Colleges** or book marking websites, let this be the moment in life when you learn how to maintain a good filing system.

Are there other resources?
In addition to the literature from each college that will inundate you, there's no shortage (and this is a good thing) of resources to help you explore your world of options while narrowing down the choices. Counselor Shaw's arse-nal includes The Princeton Review books and many other college guides from companies that work hard to help you be more informed about your college admissions choices. Most, if not all, of these organizations make their informa-tion and advice available online (one example: PrincetonReview.com), where often you can register a username and let the site guide you through the se-lection process. Among those, we highly recommend The Princeton Review's "Counselor-o-Matic," which asks you to plug in everything from your SAT/ACT scores to study interests to the parts of the country you'd like to zone in on—all of which are factored into list of schools that you might fancy.

Throughout all this, don't panic. You'll find the right college. It may even find you first. Counselor Cynthia Martini encourages you to stay "open-minded. Do not lock into one school. Look to see what it is that you may really like about that school and then look for several schools that fit that kind of pro-file." But even before that, Martini tells her students to give her "a 'picture' of their dream school." Counselor Esther Walling allows three dream schools on a student's list. And those, along with "three stretches" and "three sure-things," should be the ones you commit to visiting in the summer. Because once you've gone from virtual campus tour to actual campus tour, your gut will start to guide you, too.

ENLIST & ENROLL?

What are my college opportunities via the armed forces?

Zachary, freshman, Alabama, considering military school and wants to go into engineering

"Be all that you can be." Or is it an "Army of One?" Or, more simply, "Go Army?" Either which way, you've probably seen a poster or bumper sticker stating just that in the past few years. Joining the army (or any of the other armed services for that matter) is a very viable option for many students following graduation from high school. The reasons for enlisting can vary, but usually fall into one of three categories: the student is looking at being a career soldier; the student is enlisting as a way to pay for college after the term of service is over; or the student is at a loss for what to do with life and just wants some time to figure it all out while earning some cash and (perhaps) traveling the world.

Can my counselor advise me when it comes to the armed forces?

That's an interesting question. Many don't know because they've never really been exposed to it, but most agree that you should look toward those who have experience with the military way of life. This is not an unusual response. Recruiters don't visit every high school campus, some school districts don't invite them for career day, and some towns are so small and remote that there are no recruiter's offices within a reasonable distance for the student to visit. Given this, many counselors can be at a loss when asked about such opportunities since there is an absolute abundance of specialties available. In fact, virtually any job that is found in the civilian world is represented in the army, and then some.

For this reason, a soldier's job while serving may very well translate into gainful employment on the outside. For example, most police departments jump at the chance to hire veterans thanks to their skill set. But you need to ask yourself some frank questions before you jump in. Particularly, is this what you really want? Counselor Debra Holmes-Brown puts it this way, "I always ask if they have thought about all angles of the military—is it their choice, and are they doing this because they want to, or is it because of the immediate benefits such as lodging, food, medical coverage, etc." As an "expert" on admission to military academies, Susan M. Patterson says, "I interview very strictly those who say they want to attend to make sure their priorities are in order (not just for free tuition and the 'glory'). Insofar as enlisting, I talk very realistically with both students and parents about what to expect and the benefits and downside of the military experience."

This is a responsible approach. It must be established that the student understands that along with all those great benefits comes a lot of hard work, the very real chance of being put in harm's way, and the sobering knowledge that the commitment is real. Unlike civilian jobs, you can't just submit a resignation letter if things turn less than rosy. To do so means serving real time in the lock-up and a tarnished record forever. On the other hand, if this is something that you are committed to, there are valuable intangibles. Even after serving one tour of duty, showing military experience on a résumé signals to future employers that the veteran has leadership and discipline skills. Some employers also give veterans extra credit points that non-vets don't get.

Make sure you talk to your family first. "I believe this is an issue that parents and their children should discuss," says Diane E. Epstein of College Planning Service, Inc. As stated above, military service entails risks not found in many civilian jobs, and it's important that you let your loved ones know as they more than likely have a heavily-vested interest in your well-being. Overall, there are worse choices you could make. Dr. Dean Skarlis, president of The College Advisor of New York says, "It is an excellent option for some students. There are

FROM THE COUNSELORS

"For a kid who loves technology and who can't afford to pay a college, the military can save some people financially, but I always point out the risks. I had one disadvantaged kid who got a full ride to Wellesley, but couldn't afford to take it...She did the Harvard general studies program, while sustaining a full-time job. It took her 10 years, but she did it. I'd take that over the military, but I never close the door on any idea."

–Donald Dunbar
Founder and consultant
Dunbar Educational Consultants, LLC

many factors that are specific to the student and family, so it totally depends on the family."

What is the best way to prepare?

If you are leaning toward enlisting in the army following graduation, you will find it useful to prepare as thoroughly as possible. What's the best way to do this? In an ideal situation, your school offers the Reserve Officers' Training Corps (ROTC). Joining and participating will go a long way toward familiarizing yourself with the traditions, customs, duties, and life in the army. Boot camp comes as a bit of a shock in the best of circumstances, but experience in the ROTC will soften the blow somewhat.

How else should you prepare? In general, counselors suggest that you should concentrate in a curriculum focused on history, math, and physical activity. Studying foreign languages is also a huge asset, given the global nature of today's military.

"It is an excellent option for some students. There are many factors that are specific to the student and family, so it totally depends on the family."

—Dr. Dean P. Skarlis
President
The College Advisor of New York

"I first determine why the military is under consideration. We would look at all military options including academies and ROTC. If the interest is in the military itself and other options have not presented themselves, then I encourage the student and parents to consider ROTC or at the least attending college while in the military."

—Donnamarie Hehn
Director of college guidance
Canterbury School of Florida

MIND THE GAP

Should I take time off after high school?

Olivia, junior, Maryland, does well in English but not in math, and she plans on staying close to her home and her boyfriend who is a sophomore

What's a gap year, you ask? For one, it's a term far more common in Europe and Australia than in the United States, but it has steadily been gaining recognition here over the past few years. A gap year is what you call taking some time off between graduating from high school and starting college. What might you do with this time? Travel the world, volunteer to build houses, teach kids, work on a farm, help the elderly, work on an inner-city project, learn how to build guitars, become an apprentice cobbler, teach yourself Esperanto, work in the big city, help with family needs—actually, you could do any or all of the above.

Why might you want to do this? Maybe just to catch a breather from academics for a while or maybe to decide if college is really for you; perhaps you need a little time to figure out what you want to study or maybe you just want to work and save money for your studies. When it comes down to it, your reasons for considering a gap year, and what to do with it, will be as individual as you are.

FROM THE COUNSELORS

"Make sure you go into your gap year with a goal toward developing self-knowledge, skills, and a career. A gap year is a huge opportunity to explore and get to know who one is presently and what you seek to become."

–Angela Conley
College admissions manager
Sponsors for Educational Opportunity

"Have a plan."

–Christine Asmussen
Director of college counseling
St. Andrew's-Sewanee School

Counselors have varied ideas and advice about the idea of a gap year. "Good idea!" says counselor Autumn Luscinski. "If a student is thinking of it, they probably realize that they need another year of maturity." On the other hand, assistant principal Teresita Wardlow and counselor H. Allen Wrage, Jr. are among those who advise succinctly, "Don't do it." Educational consultant Joan Tager's opinion falls somewhere between these: "Depends on the kid and the parents and the reasons for the gap year. No blanket advice for this sticky wicket." However, counselor Barbara Yeager has a more transitory idea. "I am not a fan of the gap year," she says. "I'd rather students wait and take a semester or year to study abroad or do an internship after they're 21. Students will be more mature by then." Counselor Alicia Curry advises, "Go ahead and enter college that first year. Otherwise, you may never go."

That said, director of college guidance Ann Harris and many other counselors think taking a gap year can be a really good idea though. "Please do," says Harris. "There are so many great places to go, so many volunteer opportunities to undertake. At our school the expectation of most every parent is that their child will go directly to a four-year university and get started on college. Some aren't really ready." The College Connection director Suzan Reznick agrees. "I advise that for many students it is indeed a wonderful idea [to take a gap year]," she says.

How do I plan for it?

If you're interested in taking some time off, counselors have suggestions regarding how to plan for it and how to plan around that not-going-back-to-school trap. First of all, "You should do something you are passionate about during the gap year," says The College Scout's consultant Alison Cotten. This is true whether you are working, traveling, volunteering, or all of the above,

"A gap year is wonderful idea, but only if you have a plan in place before you enter into the year. Apply to colleges in the fall of your senior year along with your classmates as most colleges will readily defer your seat for a year."

—Rebecca Threewitt
College counselor
The King's Academy

counselors point out, because you want the gap year to be a great part of your life, and you also want it to be a great part of your college admission plan, too. (Seriously, think about how good some of those experiences will look on your application.) And you should talk with college representatives about that. "Visit with colleges that you are interested in and explain what you are doing and what do they recommend for keeping yourself current," advises director of guidance Bruce Richardson. "Make sure you have a comprehensive plan that entails the end result of such a hiatus," adds Academic Directions' president Barry Sysler. He gives an example of how to do that. "In other words," he says, "if a student wants to involve himself in an internship or apprenticeship in the city, such employment will make that student more marketable to a college as a result of such employment."

Ann Montgomery, consultant for Sage Educational Group, recommends this approach: "It's almost always best to apply to college before taking the year off. It's hard to send in applications from a yurt in Mongolia!" Wherever your gap year plan may take you, even if it's to a job in your hometown, many counselors agree it's best to apply while still in school. Colleges often allow deferred admission (starting your studies at a later date than you had at first applied for). Investigating this can be a really good idea, counselors agree. "Do all your applications in senior year when you have the resources available to you and then defer admission to your college of choice," says guidance director Andrea Badger. Getting your applications taken care of while you have resources such as references, transcripts, and counselors as part of your daily life increases the likelihood that things will go smoothly. Plus, knowing that you'll have a spot in college in the future will ease any concerns your parents, your counselors, and maybe even you may have about returning to school after your gap year's done. A side benefit is that talking about your gap year plans with college representatives gives them a chance to know more about you, and also you to know more about the college, which should help when it comes time to move back into academic life.

So should you take a gap year? You're the only one who can decide if it's the right choice for you. Nancy W. Cadwallader, consultant for Collegiate Advisory Placement Service, puts things in perspective with this advice: "Do a gap year to enrich your academic and personal profile—don't do it just to be doing a gap year."

CAMPUS CONSIDERATIONS

What do I look for during college visits?

Aaron, sophomore, Utah, has had substance abuse problems and is looking to study something agricultural at a small school in a rural setting

You'll want to check out all kinds of things while you are there. "I think the visit to campus is vital as a student needs to see the facilities and meet the students, faculty, and staff," says director of college counseling Sarah Soule. "I think they should also plan time to visit the surrounding area so they can see what the town or city is like." A suburb might be a welcoming neighborhood or labyrinth of track housing; a city can provide a rush of energy or rush hour headaches; and a rural campus might be peaceful and reflective or feel like it's located at the end of the world. You need to reflect on how you perceive things on and off campus, and why. "The visit is incredibly important," says counselor Mary Kovis Watson.

College advisor Helene Kunkel asks you to ask yourself the following. "Would you buy a car without seeing it or test driving it? Don't you usually look at the menu in a restaurant before you order? Why wouldn't you take the same care with a choice that you will want to live with for four years?" She also points out that to get the clearest picture of what to expect, you should visit when school is in session, not during breaks or holidays. "The visit is important because it does give a student that 'how does it feel' opportunity," says director of college counseling Barbara Simmons. Feeling adventurous or just chatty by nature? "Sit in the student center for a while and talk randomly with students," recommends educational consultant Nancy P. Masland. Ronna Morrison, an independent counselor, agrees: "It's very important to visit when a college is in session. If possible, do an overnight visit (particularly if considering early decision) and talk to many students, not just a tour guide."

Are college visits really necessary?

Yes, if you can, and before you even apply, if you can swing it. There are things about the campus vibe—and the surrounding town—that you just won't get second hand. After all, those glossy college brochures can only take you so far.

According to Petrequin College Consulting's Marilyn Petrequin, it's "critical" to visit colleges you're interested in. "Look at the students," she advises, "visit a class, stay overnight if possible. You will live there the next four years so you have to decide if it is right for you." Independent educational consultant Dr. Laurie H. Nash agrees: "I insist that my students visit a wide range of schools when selecting schools that are appropriate for them to apply. I always tell them to look at the students when making a decision." If you go to that school, you'll be one of its students. Can you picture yourself there? How well do you like that picture?

It is "crucial not only for the student to understand the advantages of this particular college, but at many schools, not visiting works against the student in the admissions process," says educational consultant Nancy Gore Marcus. "Whenever possible, we say visit! We have a page of questions a student can take with her when visiting a college," says Barbara Simmons. Whether or not your counselor offers one, it's a good idea to have your own checklist, and to carry along notebook and a camera to help you remember what you learn—trust us, the hectic nature of college visits will leave you wishing you had more time to notice things. "A campus visit is crucial!" says academic counselor Ruth K. Littlefield. "Be careful not to get blinded by the amazing marketing done by schools. Speak to all sorts of students, especially those that are not hired by the school to be tour guides!" That said, you'll want to pick up any

FROM THE COUNSELORS

"The campus visit is the most important part of selecting a college. Almost every college has admissions material that makes it seem like a good choice, and all campuses have their share of great professors, but feeling like you can fit in is just as important."

–Rachel Elkins Thompson
Director of educational counseling
Douglas L. Thompson, CPA PLLC

"It's very important to visit when a college is in session. If possible, do an overnight visit (particularly if considering early decision) and talk to many students, not just a tour guide."

–Ronna Morrison
Independent counselor

literature that's available, and look for things that may not be given to you, such student publications, town newspapers, and the like.

What if my parents want to go?

If you are visiting along with your parents or other students, plan time so each of you can go off for a while on your own and then meet up later—this way you'll be able to focus on the aspects of the campus that appeal to you. "The campus visit is important for students," says Educational Options' director Renee L. Goldberg. "If they cannot visit before applying, visiting at least a few colleges to which they are accepted is critical. I encourage students to look at bulletin boards and talk with students in the cafeteria." This brings up a good point—don't forget to relax while you're on campus. Don't be afraid to kick back for a moment or two and collect your thoughts—you might notice something new or unexpected. After all, had Newton not taken a break under that apple tree, who knows where we'd be now?

"The campus visit is essential. Students should keep in mind that the admissions office is trying to sell the college. A student should try to observe the everyday actions of the students they meet, such as whether students are smiling when they walk across campus."

—Kate McVey
Director of college advising
Brebeuf Jesuit Preparatory School

COLLEGE VISIT BLUES

What can I do if I don't have the cash to do a campus visit?

Joe, senior, Connecticut, works part time and is planning on needing significant financial aid

Many students have dreams of attending a college far from home, either in the big city, near the beach, or on the other side of the country. But traveling to visit colleges, especially several all at once, can be very expensive. With fuel costs on the rise, even visits to in-state colleges that may be only a few hours away by car can add up, especially if the student is interested in seeing many schools before deciding to make the commitment to fill out the application. Nevertheless, nothing can quite replace an in-person visit to a college to help the student to develop a gut feeling about whether or not he or she could be happy there for the next four years.

For this reason, it is important to figure out an alternative way to get a sense of a college before applying if money is tight, and later, to find some method of visiting colleges that you're seriously considering attending after the acceptance letters come in. Independent counselor Valerie Broughton explains

FROM THE COUNSELORS

"Go with friends. Ask to stay in the dorms. Use Amtrak college travel discounts. Visit after acceptance."

–Scott White
Director of guidance
Montclair High School

"Take advantage of local programs offered by colleges at hotel receptions and meet with any representatives who visit our school in the fall. Do careful research in guidebooks and on college websites. Be sure to have a local interview, if one is offered. Contact colleges to see if there are any free or low-cost programs to bring prospective students to campus in the fall of senior year. Travel with friends' families who are visiting colleges that interest you."

–Letitia W. Peterson
Co-director of college counseling
Holton-Arms School

her advice about college visits: "I tell students to develop an e-mail relationship with the admissions representative covering our geographic area and explain. Be up front. I advise [students] to tell the admissions folks that they've done a careful search, have chosen that school to apply to based on everything they've learned but that they can't afford to visit until they get their acceptance letter. My advice: You can apply to a college you haven't visited, but you can't send a deposit until you've visited. Also, find out if a college will support an applicant's travel costs as some will."

This general outline for visiting is advised by many counselors. When deciding whether or not to apply to a college, there are many ways to get a feel for whether or not that school will might make a good fit without visiting in person. Shirley Bloomquist, an independent college counselor, says, "The next best thing to a campus visit is reading The Fiske Guide and The Princeton Review's The Best 371 Colleges book. Then talk to students [attending the college], your high school counselor, and college reps."

What about online tours?

In this age of technology, you can get a pretty good idea of what a campus is like without even leaving the house. Every college or university has an official website, and many offer virtual tours. Blogs and social networking websites, such as Facebook, can give a realistic, if not always flattering, picture of student life on campuses you're interested in. Certified educational planner Farron Peatross suggests that students "use the Internet, college websites, and college student chat rooms, and also e-mail with professors to try to get a feel for the college experience on that campus."

"Ask others to help you out. Invite them to go with you. And also don't feel ashamed to ask the admissions office if they provide any transportation vouchers."

—Trey Chappell
Director
College X-ing, LLC

Still, it's probably a good idea to try to get some time in with a real person associated with the schools you're interested in. Lead counselor Ellen E. Underwood suggests to her students, "Do all you can online, [but then] see if there is a way to connect with some students who attend the college you are interested in who live in your area when they are home on breaks." In fact, there are some colleges and universities that recommend or require interviews as part of the application process. It may be possible to arrange an interview even if you can't physically make it to campus. If finances are limited, certified educational planner Suzanne F. Scott recommends her students "be frank and open with colleges about that, and hopefully, arrange for alumni/ae off campus interviews." Independent counselor Sandra Bramwell-Riley offers another solution for students who need to interview but can't afford the costs associated with visiting at the application stage. She suggests students "send in a résumé and set a phone appointment."

Do I go before or after the acceptance letter?

After you've received acceptances, it's extremely important to visit the campuses you actually might attend before you make the final decision. There is a vast difference between not being able to afford a lot of visits to many campuses all at once, and not being able to afford a single visit to the school you plan to attend. Director of college counseling Carol A. London notes, "If they can't afford the travel costs to visit, there would be the same issue if they attended the school. That is why location is important in considering options."

However, if you receive many acceptances and would like to visit several schools in the short time before you must commit to a single college, there may be ways to cut the cost. Tracy Spann, an independent counselor, says, "Some colleges offer travel scholarships. I encourage students who demonstrate financial need to contact the admissions office to find if such scholarships are available." Counselor Sharon F. Drell says, "If you get admitted by a college far away, they may fly you out to visit. Most schools have some type of funding and certain weekends for visits by less fortunate students. If they really want you to attend, they will find a way. Or, we can sometimes get a business in the area to sponsor the student. He or she can always fundraise."

IS BIG BROTHER WATCHING YOU?

Will my personal stuff online impact my college admissions chances?

Jessica, junior, Washington D.C., is involved in student government and wants to design her own major

Facebook, Xanga, Bebo, LiveJournal—chances are, you and your friends are on one or more of these or other equally popular social networking sites. Chances are, too, that you mainly see these sites as places to hang out online with your friends, to stay in touch, to share jokes and frustrations and general life comments, and maybe, to push the boundaries a bit—or a lot. You may think of these posts as private conversations, but keep in mind you can't dictate who sees what once you post something online. It might surprise you to learn that some of the people who could be reading what you said about last weekend's party—or worse—could be the very people who will be making decisions about your college admission prospects.

It's not that they're looking up every applicant, but it might be a question of how lucky you feel. A recent **USA Today** story reported that more than 25 percent of college admissions officers regularly research applicants through their profiles on social networking sites. Are you willing to accept those kinds of odds? "I think college admissions reps do look at these more often than students realize," says director of college counseling Sarah Soule. "I would hope that colleges make the decision based on academic information, but a poor profile on Facebook or MySpace can reflect on the student in an ill way." "I have heard that schools have looked at these profiles," says counselor Mary Kovis Watson. "I can imagine there would be some impact, otherwise they wouldn't be looking."

Can a school look at my profile if I don't include the information on my application?

Some students include information from their online pages in the application portfolios, and if you're going to do that, it's a wise idea to make sure that everything about you online reflects your good judgment and maturity. Even if you don't call attention to your online presence, someone else might, or college admissions staff might go looking anyway. "More frequently, college admissions officers have been telling our students that postings on the web might come into play with how the students are viewed," reports director of college counseling Barbara Simmons.

Increasingly, college admissions offices have established presences on social networking sites, though they're mainly there to answer questions. "To my knowledge, college admissions officers do not look at Facebook or MySpace profiles unless a student mentions the site in the application," says director of educational counseling Rachel Elkins Thompson. "I don't think the site has any impact." Director of college advising Kate McVey says, "I think college admissions officers look at Facebook or MySpace stuff when it is given to them. I don't think most of them have the time to go out and search for students." She points out, though, that she discourages students from putting personal information online. "We tell our students to make sure that their postings are never questionable," adds Barbara Simmons. "Students should be careful with what they put on the internet," advises counselor Ruth K. Littlefield. "I let my students know that there is a chance of schools looking at Facebook or MySpace."

FROM THE COUNSELORS

"I think college admissions reps do look at these more often than students realize. I would hope that colleges make the decision based on academic information, but a poor profile on Facebook or MySpace can reflect on the student in an ill way."

—Sarah Soule
Director of college counseling
Vermont Commons School

"We've heard that college admissions officers do look at those profiles—and we tell our students to make sure that their postings are never questionable."

—Barbara Simmons
Director of college counseling
Notre Dame High School

Regardless of whether you think that it's right for college officers to be checking out your online profile, you have to accept that they may be doing so. As many college students, celebrities, and high-powered investment bankers have found out, a seemingly funny posting online can come back to haunt you in a big way. So while you're getting your application material ready, it might be a good idea to give your online pages a good look, too—only this time from the perspective of the admissions office. If you didn't know the person represented by this page, what would you think? Would you invest in his or her future?

"To my knowledge, college admissions officers do not look at Facebook or MySpace profiles unless a student mentions the site in the application. I don't think the site has any impact."

–Rachel Elkins Thompson
Director of educational counseling
Douglas L. Thompson, CPA PLLC

Chapter 2
Academics, Extracurriculars, & Everything in Between

MIDDLE SCHOOL VS. HIGH SCHOOL

What changes academically between middle school and high school?

Isaac, 8th grader, Montana, is deciding whether to request being moved up to honors classes next year, wants to be more challenged in high school than he was in middle school

Whether you're looking ahead or looking back, you know there's a big difference between where you are as a freshman in high school and where you are, or will be, as a senior. You face all sorts of changes, decisions, and opportunities in these years. It goes without saying that high school will be a different world from what you've known in middle school. But how different will it be? Obviously the social scene will change. But what do you need to know about the academic differences?

"In middle school, students are given many more chances and opportunities to complete work or do work over to show their best. In high school, it is expected that they are doing their best work when they turn it in," points out guidance coordinator Bruce Barrett. "Middle school teachers tend to coddle students," says guidance department head Barbara Bayley. "My experiential response suggests that middle schools, with the exception of private secondary environments, are typically not as intellectually challenging" as high school, says

FROM THE COUNSELORS

"[In high school], the work load is heavier, students have more choice in their curriculum, and students must take more responsibility for completing their work, asking for help, and learning the material."

—Barbara Pasalis
Principal
Northcoast Educational Consulting

college admissions manager Angela Conley. "The kids are younger and less focused [in middle school]," says educational consultant Joan Tager. "The boys are extremely hyper, while girls tend to be more developed and somewhat more mature." She also adds that even in middle school, students "must be on the right math and foreign language tracks for selective colleges." This goes to show how important academics are in preparation for college—the earlier you start working toward it, the better prepared you'll be for it.

Will I need skills from middle school?

"Middle school is for skill-building in reading, writing and math," says counselor Barbara Yeager. "It's a very important time!" Why is it so important, you ask? Well, it's a time when you have the chance to begin to develop good study and organizational habits—a time for laying the academic groundwork for some successful high school years. According to counselor H. Allen Wrage, middle school is "more nurturing" to students as compared to high school. "High school requires more academic independence for students," says college consultant Alison Cotten. "Late or missing assignments, for example, always have consequences that are tied to grades, and many students are surprised at this after having been carried along by sympathetic middle school teachers." High school classes typically involve more reading, writing, and research than you ever thought about in middle school. It's not just information gathering or repeating back what you read, either. There's "more critical thinking [required] in high school," says assistant principal Teresita Wardlow.

"I describe high school as varsity. It is more of an independent learning experience. You are taught in school, but you learn at home."

—Antonios Lazaris
Secondary school counselor
East Hampton High School

Will I get to be more independent?

Despite the increased workload and emphasis on self-reliance, high school doesn't have to be grim or heavy duty. If you've not already had the chance to try out being a self-motivated student, you'll get to do that, and if you're already independent-minded in academics, high school will give you new challenges. "Oh, my goodness—middle school and high school are worlds apart," says director of college counseling Christine Asmussen. "We expect our upper school students to be more independent and to work at a much deeper level with the material." Guidance director Andrea Badger agrees. "More independent, self-motivated work is needed in high school." There is also "far more peer pressure and more uncertainty about the caliber of academic challenge," adds Angela Conley. "There's more independence for the student and less help given unless asked for—meaning that students must be their own advocates in high school," says educational consultant Nancy W. Cadwallader. But don't worry—you won't be caught too off guard. "High school is to prepare you for college, whereas middle school is to prepare you for high school," says Carla Cruz.

COUNTDOWN TO GRADUATION

What should I be doing in the 9th, 10th, 11th, and 12th grades to prepare for college admissions?

Jocelyn, 8th grader, West Virginia, is an overachiever, wants to work for NASA

With the lazy days of junior high behind you, you have only a precious three or four years of school until graduation...and then college. For some students, the decision to attend college after high school is a given—they've always known they wanted to head to college, so it's the next logical step. For others, there can be some uncertainty due to academics, scheduling, and financial situations. Regardless of which camp you fall into, high school is the perfect time to examine what you want to do with your future and prepare for it at the same time. What might you want to study? Where do you want to go to school? What if you don't get accepted at your first choice college? Will you go straight into college from high school or take a little time off? How will you pay for college? Is college even right for you? The list goes on, but here are some suggestions to help you streamline the process.

What should some of my goals be?

Whether you're a freshman or a senior, counselors recommend you focus on getting good grades, staying organized and studying, getting involved in extracurriculars, and developing skills that'll serve you well regardless of whichever path you choose to take in life. "Take a challenging academic curriculum, develop strong writing and analytical thinking skills, cultivate strong study habits, pursue interests, and get involved seriously in at least one activity," advises counselor Christine Asmussen.

Counselor Joan Tager recommends using the 9th and 10th grades to focus on "defining a passion" and following this through in your "course selection." Taking a wide variety of classes will go a long way in helping you decide what interests you have and where your talents lie. In the 10th and 11th grades, standardized test preparation is essential. Bruce Barrett recommends that high school students "take a rigorous course load, do their best in each class, focus on a few other activities that they can [get deeply involved] in, and save money." Trust us on the saving money part—one thing you'll quickly discover once you get to college is that the living, while fun, ain't cheap, and there are only so many nights in a row you can eat ramen noodles.

Can I at least take the summers off?

Don't forget about those months between spring and fall either. While it's tempting to do nothing but soak up some sun all day long, the summer is the perfect time to pursue "programs related to your passions," says Joan Tager. Internships, camps, study-abroad programs, even a 9-to-5 job at the local ice cream shop can play an important role in helping you figure out not only what you might like to study at college, but also what you might want to do in life (not to mention earn a little pocket money while serving sundaes).

Barbara Yeager agrees that all four school years and the summers included are the best time to explore your options and interests. "Pursue the most challenging courses available," she says. "Find venues where you can shine as a leader or significant participant. Gain context on your world through community service by giving back, as well as participating in summer academic or travel programs." How about something you can do without having to leave your house? "Read more," says Suzan Reznick, "especially outside of school assignments."

What if I don't know what to do?

There are tons of opportunities to get involved no matter what your interests—and it's worth investigating them all! Here is a list of the seven general

FROM THE COUNSELORS

"In the 9th and 10th grades, students should focus on their academics and work to understand their interests, strengths, and talents. They should also build an extracurricular résumé. The first two years are for students to gain self-understanding. The college search begins in earnest in 11th grade. A college list should be developed early in the year so that all college visits can be completed by the end of the school year and applications can be worked on over the summer. In the 12th grade, students should focus on the all-important first semester courses; in the winter, they can research and apply for merit scholarship opportunities."

—Barbara Palasis
Principal
Northcoast Educational Consulting

categories of extracurricular activities according to the Forum for Youth Investment's "Out-of-School Time Commentary Series":

- Academic support/mentoring (after school programs that place an emphasis on academics)

- Service-learning (volunteer experience)

- Youth empowerment/organizing (programs that give students the opportunity to form organizations that employ valuable academics skills such as critical thinking and research)

- Employment/career development (mentor-driven internships in a variety of professions)

- Recreation (a wide array of sports and athletics)

- Prevention (a combination of after-school programs, which serve to encourage students to support a healthy lifestyle)

- Culture, arts, and media (a series of programs that challenge students to use artistic mediums to express their ideas and perspectives)

Ultimately, Rebecca Threewitt sums it up this way: "Each year should build on the last, both in academics and extracurricular activities. Students should be challenging themselves with the most advanced subjects that are available to them. Just as important, though, is finding a passion and developing skills."

"High school should not just be viewed as a springboard for college, or [students] will miss out. [It's a time to] try to find out what your real interests and personal strengths are. Don't only pursue the areas that you are good at—take some academic and extracurricular risks."

—Suzan Reznick
Director
The College Connection

PREPARATION MAKES PERFECT

What can I do in high school to prepare for success in college?

Camila, 8th grader, South Carolina, is studying hard for the PSAT, and she will be a first-generation student

Forms, deadlines, essays, recommendations, finances, choices, decisions, tests, interviews—there are lots and lots of details you'll be wading through when you apply to college. But what happens when you actually get there? It'll be a new and exciting and sometimes unfamiliar scene that will be your academic and social world for the next few years. Beyond all the details of applying and getting accepted and paying for college, what are the best things you can be doing while still in high school to get ready to face life as a college student?

"Students need to understand that they need to work hard," says counselor Mary Kovis Watson. "Tough classes in high school, where they have to do extensive reading and writing (and rewriting), are probably the best preparation [for college academics]." "Rigorous high school courses and strong reading and writing skills [are important]," says independent counselor Ronna

FROM THE COUNSELORS

"Students need to take academically-challenging courses starting their freshman year of high school. They also need to read."

—Nannette Umeda
Post-secondary counselor
Kaiser High School

"I think having a well-rounded education where a student has the opportunity to learn about success and failure in the classroom and in extracurricular pursuits is the best preparation a student can have for college."

—Rachel Elkins Thompson
Director of educational counseling
Douglas L. Thompson, CPA PLLC

Morrison. Start early with this plan, advises counselor Nannette Umeda. "Students need to take academically-challenging courses starting their freshman year of high school," she says. "They also need to read." She isn't alone on this point. Most, if not all, counselors agree that you shouldn't read only when you have homework. "Reading outside of school" is a habit that will pave the way to success in college, says Educational Options director Renee L. Goldberg.

Should I fill out my application without any help?

High school is not just about studying and reading, either. College advisor Helene Kunkel says that you should "Internalize your resolve to resist peer pressure." She adds, "When you get to college, the opportunities to mess up are endless! Do much of the application process yourself, without parental help, because you will need to [learn how to] be independent in college." High school can be a time to begin to learn about what you value, who you are, and how you handle independence. Some of this may have already come to you naturally through your school and family situations, and some you may have to think about, or decide to develop.

What's the best piece of advice?

"I think having a well-rounded education where a student has the opportunity to learn about success and failure in the classroom and in extracurricular pursuits is the best preparation a student can have for college," says Douglas L. Thompson's director of educational counseling, Rachel Elkins Thompson. "Be willing to learn and remember your priorities. Have fun and try new things but stay focused on school work," says academic counselor Ruth K. Littlefield. "Motivation, determination, and good study habits" are the three things

"There are many 'best preparations' for college, but among them, knowing oneself, knowing one's strengths and one's challenges can help students not only seek help once at college, but also look closely at what colleges will fit best."

—Barbara Simmons
Director of college counseling
Notre Dame High School

independent educational consultant Dr. Laurie H. Nash sees as most important for college success, and they are all things you can find ways to work on, learn about, and put into practice during high school.

"Engagement in academics, exploration of content, interest and creativity, and a strong desire to be successful" are the key ingredients in the recipe for a great college experience, says director of college counseling Sarah Soule. "There are many 'best preparations' for college, but among them, knowing oneself, knowing one's strengths and one's challenges can help students not only seek help once at college, but also look closely at what colleges will fit best," points out director of college counseling Barbara Simmons.

Isn't all this hard work just to impress admissions committees?

Counselors agree that challenging yourself academically in high school is a good idea, not just for what you can learn, and not just to impress college admissions officers, but for what you'll learn about yourself. Learning about yourself, what makes you tick, what stresses you out (and how you handle that), knowing how you handle responsibility and manage time—these are just a few of the things you can learn about yourself as you get ready for college, if you take the time, as counselors suggest, to get to know yourself better. And here's one more quality that you should be sure you take along with you, too: "Resilience," says educational consultant Nancy P. Masland. You may not come out of every situation college throws at you smelling like roses—in fact, some may leave you wondering why you ever bothered applying—but if you can get back on your feet and keep at it, you'll see everything pay off in spades.

ROOM FOR IMPROVEMENT

What can I do if my grades aren't so hot?

Laura, senior, Tennessee, has a C average in classes that aren't
challenging, but she has lots of extracurriculars, including
dance team, and she wants to go to the University of Tennessee
to study communications

Grades. Arguably, it's all about the grades when it comes to scoring a spot at a good college—or at least they're the most important part of the equation when it comes to getting in. Good grades can lead to a good college, a good college looks good on your résumé, and a good-looking résumé makes it a lot easier to find a good job in our increasingly competitive economy. So what's this story's moral? Grades are important—good or bad, they matter, but bad grades will end up hurting you in all the ways good ones won't.

What to do if you have poor grades? It's time to light a fire under them and heat them up. Don't think that just because your grades are low everything's lost. Most college admissions offices look favorably on students who start off poorly but then work to raise their grades. Lead counselor Carrie Boettger says, "I think admissions staff will look at this situation positively."

What if I don't have time to study?
Crack the books and study anyway. That sounds obvious, doesn't it? Sometimes the simplest solution is the best. There are a lot of reasons that you probably don't log enough study time. You might have a part-time job. You might be helping the family budget or you might just be working to pay for your car insurance. Either way, you'll need to find more time to study. Get up earlier, stay up later, cut back on working hours, or even dedicate the weekend to the books—you'll thank yourself later.

What if I want to focus more on my extracurriculars?
Another problem keeping you from your best grades might be a conflict of priorities. Odd as it may seem, there are parts of the country where football is king. It actually takes priority over academic achievement. Case in point, some

time ago, Texas legislators passed a regulation dubbed "No Pass, No Play." It was quite simple: if you don't pass your classes, you don't get to play football. You would expect Bubba the quarterback to object (you know the guy, he buys his term papers and is sure he's going to the NFL), but the surprising thing is the amount of parents that raised a fit! They actually cared more about junior's high school glory days than they did about the future forty years of earning power. Go figure. If you're into sports, don't feel like you have to give up on them. Just cut back enough so that you can get those grades higher. And once you get them high, don't cut back on the time you take to study—the reason they're better is because of the time you've invested. No more time, no better grades.

What about getting a tutor?

Sometimes this is the thing that does the trick. Why? For a number of reasons. Especially in subjects like mathematics, there are times when what the high school math teacher is saying just doesn't connect and make sense. As the math course work gets to a more difficult and abstract level, communication between you and your teacher becomes increasingly critical. When you learned addition, those fingers came in handy because there are 10 of them. That crutch doesn't work with calculus. This is where a tutor comes in. You might just need concepts explained from a different angle on a more personal level.

Are study groups helpful?

Study groups can also be a very effective technique to bring up your grades. In one sense, it's like the tutor approach, but it's usually free, so your wallet can breathe a sigh of relief. Another benefit is that since it's a social event with

FROM THE COUNSELORS

"Generally, an upward trend in grades is looked upon positively."

—Dr. Dean P. Skarlis
President
The College Advisor of New York

"Many colleges, excluding the most competitive, will take improving grades into account, especially if the student is ultimately taking advanced courses in at least what they consider a 'meat and potato' area: history, English, biology, physics, chemistry, and calculus."

—Donald Dunbar
Founder and consultant
Dunbar Educational Consultants, LLC

your peers, it's mentally easier to make time for studying, and you'll probably make some good friends as a result. The ideal place to meet is the library. It'll probably be the public library since school libraries tend to shut the doors when the dismissal bell rings in the afternoon. And what could be handier than all those reference books at your fingertips?

But how can I study when all that memorization is hard?

Rote learning is the old "use a bigger hammer" approach. Most students shy away from it because, let's face it, it can be boring. Memorizing is not fun, and that makes it very resistible. But take heart, it can be easier than you think. Do you take notes in history class? One good strategy is to pick out a convenient time of the day, start from the first page of your notes, and read through to the end of your notes. This means you'll have a little bit more to read every day. But on test day, the information will be so firmly embedded that it'll be hard not to ace the test!

Another technique is to use index cards. Put your facts in the form of a question on one side and write the answer on the back. Carry them with you everywhere. Whenever it's convenient, go through the deck of cards, reading the question and trying to answer them. Even if you know the answer, flip the card and read it to yourself. Your brain will anchor the data even more securely.

Using these learning techniques will help your grades rise. It's not easy work and you'll have to make time for it, but the payoff is well worth it. "Many colleges will look at the overall trend of improvement," says assistant director of guidance Elise Ackerman. "I would encourage the student to address this in a personal statement."

"There seems to be an increasing number of schools who remove freshman grades and recalculate GPA. I also include in my recommendation letter a highlight that indicates the student may have had a slow start, but (for whatever reason) improved their grades, effort, skills, etc., and I may include an explanation if warranted (such as being diagnosed with ADD, a family divorce, a difficult transition to high school, etc.). Positive grade trends are always a good sign, as well as increasing rigor in their curriculum. Of course, a less-than-stellar start may not work for the most selective schools, unless there was some horrendous, life-changing event that occurred."

—Deborah Bernstein
Director of college counseling
Forest Ridge School of the Sacred Heart

"Improvement shows dedication, ability, and perseverance. Colleges like these traits."

—Deborah C. Curtis
Guidance counselor
Massabesic High School

THE TRIALS OF TRANSFERRING

How do I enhance my college application when I've switched schools?

Emma, senior, North Carolina, transferred from a private to a public high school when her family moved, and she is trying to get into a competitive engineering program at a tech school

Different states, and even different high schools, often have their own unique grading systems, and students who transfer from another school have their old grades "translated" to conform to their new school's system. If you under-performed at the old school, it could be an uphill climb to get into the college of your choice. But there are steps you can take to mediate the situation.

Should I try to hide my not-so-stellar grades?

Our counselors agree that being upfront about past missteps, reasons behind them, and what you've done to learn from them, will help convince admissions officers to take a chance on you.

As part of the application package, a student should include a letter laying it all out, because "the question will arise anyway," says Princeton Review master tutor Glenn Ribotsky. Educational consultant Pearl Glassman adds, "I

FROM THE COUNSELORS

"Some transfer students might do better by attending a community college and estab-lishing a year of good grades and formulating their goals and objectives. Transferring can be tough, especially to a selective school."

–Janice M. Hobart
CEO
College Found

would suggest that they write an explanatory statement telling what may have caused that spotty record. Colleges evaluate these students on an individual basis."

Would writing an essay help me?

You could also address these shortcomings in an essay, if one is required. If it isn't, write one anyway—it can't hurt. "I would tell my students to have a strong senior year, and explain their ups and downs in an essay or an interview," says counselor Heather Britton-Doucette. "We would also look at schools that would look at the student as a complete package."

In this letter or essay, it's helpful to explain what the grading system was at your old school, adding details about the substance of your classes and how they compare with those at the new school. "High school students need to explain in the application what the grading systems are/were and how they are the same or different," says counselor Esther Walling. "As a UC (in the University of California network) reader, I looked at each school and how the students challenged themselves at each."

What if I'm transferring as a senior?

If you transfer, say, in time for the second half of your senior year, there's still plenty of time to rehabilitate a sub-par academic record. Both Diana Hedstrom, a counselor in Alaska, and private college consultant Freida Gottsegen suggest filling in the "spots" by taking additional courses, either at the school where you want to attend or at a community college.

"This is where the guidance letter and continued rapport with college admissions officers can help. We often take time every fall to chat with the admissions officers who visit our high school and let them know about how we weigh and translate transfer credits and such."

–John Burke
School counselor
Winchester High School

Won't transferring leave blanks in my transcript?

As for the formulas high schools use to make transfer students' grades conform, counselor Jan Freund says, "We convert all transfer transcripts to our grading scale and then weigh accordingly for GPA and rank." Adds counselor Beth Thayer: "Transfer students have to meet our credit requirements, and just like any student with a spotty transcript, we work closely with them."

Ribotsky, for one, isn't a fan of recalibrating incoming students' previous grades. "I despise weighted averages," he says. "I don't believe colleges look at them that closely. The people who developed them think that college admissions is all about the extra tenth of a point."

What if I'm transferring colleges?

Similarly, students who already are in college and are looking to transfer to another school may find that their current schools don't use the same system as the one they're trying to get into. "Colleges know how to interpret transcripts and judge classes, but transfer students need to realize that all their courses may not be accepted," says Harriet Gershman, a certified educational planner with Academic Counseling Services, Inc. Counselor Vincent McMahon adds, "College reps say not to bother dissecting the grades, as they have their own systems."

Any sure-fire advice that will help?

To boost their chances, applicants need to use old-fashioned interpersonal methods: Work closely with counselors, contact college admissions officers directly, and keep in touch with them. If you have someone on your side who could act as a benefactor or vouch for your bona fides, recruit that person as an ally.

"Do the very best you can and build a relationship with a professor who can write on your behalf," says counselor Jane Mathias. "If your most recent performance is strong, your high school transcript becomes less important."

DRUGS, DRINKING, & OTHER THINGS THAT CAN AFFECT YOUR COLLEGE ASPIRATIONS

What if I've had some trouble in high school?

Ethan, sophomore, Nevada, has had absentee issues and has been held back a grade, but he wants to clean up his act and has changed schools and his circle of friends

It goes without saying that drugs, drinking, and other things such as skipping school, not studying, or ending up in the wrong crowd can really influence your chances of getting into college. In the first place, your grades will suffer, hampering your chance to compete with other applicants. Secondly, step back and look at the situation: If you can't control your behavior while in high school, how can a college expect you to behave and perform while on campus?

If you think you're this student, and you can buckle down and perform under the loftier expectations of higher learning, it's high time to take a change of course. After all, how can you expect to prove yourself in college if you wash out of high school? Sad as it is, you have to get through one to get through the other. So, what now? Time for a new plan.

Who do I go to for help?

Game plans aren't just for football. There's a reason the school district pays your counselor. It's his or her job to guide you through the process of successfully making it through high school and into the adult life beyond, whether it's going to college, trade school, or entering another occupation. If you're having a drinking or drug problem that you suspect is affecting your performance, or even if you're in denial, you'll have to be proactive in getting the ball rolling.

In many school districts, it's against policy to allow the counselor to bring up these sensitive topics, due to legality. For example, Donnamarie Hehn, director of college guidance at Canterbury School of Florida says, "I generally cannot discuss it unless the student brings up the topic. In that case, the student and I discuss how the use and abuse of alcohol or drugs has affected their life at this point. We then honestly discuss how college with its stresses and additional freedoms will exacerbate the situation."

What if I feel uncomfortable talking about it with my counselor?

We can all feel a bit uncomfortable discussing sensitive issues with power figures. In some cases it can be so overwhelming that you just can't bring yourself to dive in the conversation pool. But many counselors are empathetic enough to sense this and guide the conversation themselves. "I have suspected some students of drug use and taken the opportunity to talk to them about some of the things they will encounter in college—without speaking of my suspicions directly," says educational consultant Emilie Hinman. "Rather I imply that they will have temptations in college and [suggest] how to avoid them."

That said, because of the legality issue that we brought up a couple of paragraphs ago, know that your counselor may not be allowed or may not want to advise you on a drug or alcohol issue. With this is mind, it might be best to go to your family first. Diane E. Epstein of College Planning Service, Inc. says that knowing this about a student would not affect how she would advise a student looking toward college. "I believe this is an issue that parents have to face," she says.

So what happens next?

Simple. You'll have to get square with your parents or guardian and request their help. To overcome these types of problems, it's common to need a bit of moral support, and your family can provide the perfect platform to build a successful bid for cleaning up and going to college. If you find yourself in the situation where your family wouldn't be comfortable with this discussion and wind up taking your college aspirations further off course, you might need another plan.

FROM THE COUNSELORS

"If [a student's] behavior has become an issue that affects their school work or relationships, I act as a personal advisor to both student and parents concerning getting help. It is my experience that this problem is only made worse by going away to college, adding increased opportunities and stress to an already vulnerable student."

–Susan M. Patterson
CEO and director of services
College Placement Consulting

First, find a new group of friends and get involved in some college-friendly extracurricular activities. These are a great way to stay busy and build your application up. Second, take a clear look at what your goals are and how your actions are impacting them. Avoid scenes and people who might take you off your path—just like the Bard said all those years ago, "To thine own self be true."

Remember that whatever the case, you're not alone if you feel you need to ask for help. Grand Canyon University conducted a recent survey of guidance counselors, asking them the most frequent reasons students under their wing asked for help. A full 65 percent reported having been approached for substance abuse issues.

"The use of drugs and alcohol is a tricky area for a school counselor. If the use of substances is interfering with a student's success in high school, that issue needs to be addressed and college advising is not the priority. If I suspect a student recreationally uses drugs and alcohol but is successful in high school, I do not focus on the drugs and alcohol issue and simply advise the student as I would all others."

—Deborah C. Curtis
Guidance counselor
Massabesic High School

DIAGNOSIS: SENIORITIS

Can't I just coast through senior year?

Angelina, senior, Connecticut, is a B student with decent SAT scores, and she plans to enroll early decision in a state school

From the juice box days of pre-K to this final year of high school, it's been a long, strange trip, to paraphrase the late, great Jerry Garcia. For a long time it didn't seem like it would ever get here. But, now, before you know it, it's sitting on your doorstep. You're a senior, and suddenly, being a senior seems like a waste of time—you're ready to move on to whatever lies after graduation. Fair enough—believe us, we've been there. But just because high school has lost its luster doesn't mean you can slack off, even if you already have a college lined up, because your grades still matter to them.

Do my senior grades really matter?

In the words of Donnamarie Hehn, "Don't fall into the trap of senioritis! Everyone knows someone whose conditional acceptance was revoked due to low grades." Consider yourself warned, but still, a little more advice can't hurt. "Throughout the time that we work together, I remind students that senior

FROM THE COUNSELORS

"Grades do matter after a student has been accepted. I have seen the warning letter that one student received when he basically stopped completing work after being accepted to college. If a student presses for a more detailed response, I will admit that if grades slip a letter grade or so, he or she will probably still be allowed to attend, but I ask the student to look at his or her personal integrity. I ask them to think about their work ethic and state that the ability to push through to the end of something with the same degree of effort says much about their character."

–Deborah C. Curtis
Guidance counselor
Massabesic High School

year grades matter," says Emily A. Snyder. "I explain to them that colleges do expect them to finish senior year academically within the same grade range on which they were accepted and that they can in fact rescind—or ask later for an explanation before deciding to rescind—their offer of admission if there is a significant drop in grades. Many acceptance letters state that the offer of admission is contingent upon the student sustaining the academic level of work on which they were accepted through graduation." However, depending on the school you've been accepted to, there may be a sliding scale of how much you can relax academically. Dr. Dean P. Skarlis states that one thing schools don't like to see is students who do "very poorly in the second semester of their senior year."

But what if this is just a scare tactic, you ask? It's just your high school trying to keep you from relaxing after so many years of French homework and science projects, you say. After all, why would a school that has accepted you drop you just for taking a little R&R your senior year? Simply put, because it shows a lack of commitment. College classes aren't for the faint of heart or character—you'll need to put in your dues and colleges want to know they're accepting someone who's in it for the long haul. "[Your grades] set the tone for your future," says counselor Donna Fiori. "It's not about being almost finished and taking time off."

So what's the best way to stay in a college's good graces during this application process?

Well, according to Donald Dunbar, it's best to have your high school in your corner. "As long as their school stays behind them, they will not lose an acceptance. But how else does one keep their school behind them, but by

"Colleges expect that the student's level of work will not decline after admission."

–Dan Crabtree
College counselor
Wheaton Academy

"Stay strong until the last day!"

–Debra Holmes-Brown
Counselor
School of Law and Business High School

staying academically interested and responsible toward the school community?" That's right, quid pro quo, kids. Be true to your school, just like the Beach Boys said, and it'll be true to you.

But how do I deal with being bored of high school?
Deborah Bernstein says that one of the best ways to stay sane is by remaining "focused and committed right up till the very end of senior year." She adds, "I also might tell [students] to look for something new and exciting to try at school (such as a new sport or the school play) that may increase interest in their school and tide them over till the end of the year." So stay busy, stay focused, and more than anything, realize that this time, while seemingly endless, is also incredibly precious—you'll look back years later and realize that you couldn't have enjoyed yourself more. After all, just because you have to stay committed doesn't mean you can't have some fun.

HIGH SCHOOL APPEAL

Do my Ivy League hopes hang on whether I go to a public or private high school?

Meg, freshman, New York, makes A's in honors and AP classes at a private school in New York City, and she wants to go to Harvard to study pre-law

Any experienced college counselor will tell you that no student is guaranteed admission to the most selective schools, particularly those in the Ivy League. The ten Ivy League colleges are Brown University, Columbia University, Cornell University, Dartmouth College, Harvard University, University of Pennsylvania, Princeton University, and Yale University. The term "Ivy League" actually refers to the athletic conference to which these 10 colleges belong, and no others. However, the term has lost much of its association with sports, and instead has come to be synonymous with academic excellence, extreme selectivity, and, to some extent, exclusivity and elitism. Surely the reputation for rigorous academics is what has given these schools the huge pool of highly qualified, excellent applicants that obligates the schools to continue to be very selective. For example, Harvard, the most selective of the Ivy League schools, accepts less than 10 percent of its applicants each year, even though nearly all applicants meet or exceed the published academic requirements for admission. There simply aren't enough seats for all the well-qualified students who apply to the Ivies.

This selectivity creates a lot of questions and debates about what a family can do to increase the chances that a student will be accepted into one of these schools. There is no consensus among college counselors about whether attending a public or a private high school is more advantageous to Ivy League admissions.

Are the Ivies even considering students from public high schools?

Ivy League schools have been working for years to combat the impression that only very wealthy, privately educated students can gain admission to their institutions. The number of public school students accepted to Ivies fluctuates, but over time, it has increased tremendously, so that now many students attending Ivy League schools come from public high schools. For this reason, many counselors think that public school students actually have a better chance at the Ivies.

One thing to consider is that the colleges compare students from similar academic backgrounds to one another in order to find applicants who have made the most of the opportunities available to them. Trey Chappell, an independent counselor, explains his reasoning: "I believe the more selective schools, like the Ivies, prefer public school students. Private high school kids usually have more competition, and Ivies also like to 'give those less fortunate a chance.'" Similarly, counselor Scott Fisch says, "I honestly believe they have a better chance coming from a public school. For example, Yale may only look at the top two or three kids from a private school, so the number four and number five students tends to get lost."

The idea that public school gives an advantage to Ivy-seeking students has everything to do with the group that these students are compared to. Since fewer public school students apply to the Ivies, they may stand out. This is why independent college counselor Jill Madenberg thinks that the student with the best chance at the Ivy League may be the applicant coming from "a public school in a remote area," since these are the types of students Ivy League schools see the fewest applications from.

Of course, there are many counselors who disagree. There are some counselors who believe that while Ivy League schools do accept more public school students than before, a private education is still an advantage to Ivy admission. For example, independent counselor Valerie Broughton says, "the rhetoric says [admissions favor public schools] but that's not my experience. Maybe

FROM THE COUNSELORS

"There is no general rule—it just depends on the appeal of the individual candidate."

–Letitia W. Peterson
Co-director of college counseling
Holton-Arms School

if the students go to very high-powered public high schools in very privileged areas they have a better chance, but not if they attend a run-of-the-mill public high school."

Would I be ready for the Ivies if I go to public high school?

The idea that the average public high school does not adequately prepare students for Ivy League academics has other adherents. For instance, Carol A. London, director of counseling services at Bishop McGuinness Catholic High School says that though she agrees there is probably not a tendency to favor private schools, "that is a mistake on the part of the Ivy League school. Typically, private schools are more demanding and provide a more rigorous curriculum that better prepares students for college level work." And though co-director of college counseling Letitia W. Peterson says, "The academic and personal characteristics of a student must be compelling, regardless of which type of school he or she attends," she also adds that "The advantage in attending a private/independent school is the additional attention from a college counselor whose sole purpose is to guide the students through the process (there is also the advantage of a more rigorous curriculum)."

Of course, counselors readily admit that these are all generalizations. Suzanne F. Scott, a certified educational planner, says, "There are no hard and fast rules...the important thing for even the most qualified student is to look beyond the Ivy League for some of the wonderful other schools where they may be equally well-suited." And independent counselor Sandra Bramwell-Riley is quick to point out that when all's said and done, "I think that it is the student that counts."

"Some [private] schools have a reputation for sending a large number of their students to the Ivy League schools, but that is probably because they have exceptional college prep classes and the students that attend are above average students with parents who can afford that education. However, with many of the Ivy League schools offering a tuition-free education for middle class families, that may change."

–Scott White
Director of guidance
Montclair High School

ARE YOU TRUE TO YOUR SCHOOL?

How does my high school's academic reputation affect my college application?

Ava, freshman, New York, is an A student at a small high school in upstate New York, putting her application up against students from New York City high schools, and she really wants to go to NYU

When you apply to college, admissions officers will be looking at all kinds of things about you—grades, test scores, extracurricular activities, community involvement, sports, arts, essays—so that they can get the clearest idea possible of the person and student that you are. One thing they'll also be looking at is your high school. How much does it matter if you're from a well-known prep school, a big city high school, or a tiny rural classroom?

Colleges are looking to admit students from varied backgrounds, so while you can't know what kind of students they're looking to admit or how impressed they'll be with your high school, know that one thing they're keen to find out is whether you used your time to the fullest. Did you challenge yourself by taking advanced or AP classes? Did you try something new? Did you coast by on the easiest classes possible so you could build up your GPA? Expect the admissions office to want to know about all of this, but then trust them to put it in context with what else they know about you and your school. And how do

FROM THE COUNSELORS

"I believe colleges look at school profiles and count lower grades from higher performing schools as equivalent to higher grades at lower performing schools."

—Gregory Rico
Counselor
Highland Park High School

"I would hope [the admissions office] looks at school profiles and takes into consideration what opportunities each student has been given at the various schools."

—Ruth K. Littlefield
Academic counselor
York High School

they find out about your school, besides word of mouth? It's called a "school profile."

According to director of college counseling Barbara Simmons, "The school profile is a gem for college admissions officers since it will show whether or not grade inflation exists (grade distribution charts are important) and it will also show SAT/ACT averages for the school against national averages." It's about putting your academic record in context, and the more a college staff knows about different high schools, the more tools they have to do this. "I am sure that many factors go into their decision," says counselor Pat Hammett. Barbara Simmons explains, "Colleges look at profiles of the schools and at the past performances of students from those schools to see if an A is really an A." "I would hope [the admissions office] looks at school profiles and takes into consideration what opportunities each student has been given at the various schools," says academic counselor Ruth K. Littlefield.

Will a college close to home know more about my high school?
One thing admissions committees really want to see is how you have challenged yourself given the courses and activities available. But whether or not colleges know about the courses your high school offered can depend. "If [the admissions office] knows the high schools in the area as they should, they can take the differences into their decisions," says counselor Marilyn Petrequin. Don't worry too much though—even if your school doesn't have the highest of profiles, there's a good chance your counselors are working to make sure colleges take notice. "We are a high performing school that does not rank," says director of college advising Kate McVey. "We spend a lot of time educating college reps about the rigor of our curriculum and the quality of our students.

"If [the admissions office] knows the high schools in the area as they should, they can take the differences into their decisions."

—Marilyn Petrequin
College counselor
Petrequin College Consulting, LLC

I think most colleges try very hard to understand the high school that the student is coming from."

So what can you do about all this? It's easy, just remember that colleges are looking for what you've done with what you have, regardless of your high school's course offerings or geographic location, so focus on excelling in your studies and activities, and you should be just fine.

VALS & SALS

Are valedictorians and salutatorians shoo-ins for college?

George, senior, Louisiana, is the salutatorian in the Ninth Ward of New Orleans, and he wants to go to school in Boston for industrial design

There are certain students who have made getting top grades their priority from the first day of kindergarten. Many of these students are under the impression that if they can get straight A's while taking a heavy load of Advanced Placement or International Baccalaureate classes, and end up at the top of their class, they will be guaranteed a spot at a prestigious, top-ranked college and their future success will be set in stone. We won't lie—if this is the case, their chances are better than average. But still, nothing's guaranteed.

While earning the title of valedictorian or salutatorian is indeed a great accomplishment, it isn't necessarily the determining factor in college admissions. College counselors are unanimous in their proclamation that academic success, while very important, is not enough on its own to ensure a student will get into a highly ranked school. Independent counselor Tracy Spann explains, "While it is a high honor to be named valedictorian or salutatorian, the academic curriculum, test scores, and extracurricular involvement paint the complete picture of the student. College admissions officers are attempting to create a community of students with a diverse array of interests and strengths, all of which are demonstrated or revealed by the student's extra curricular involvement."

There's a major concern among college counselors that the competition for the titles of valedictorian and salutatorian has become overly intense, and it causes some students to put too much emphasis on grades. Certified educational planner Farron Peatross notes that "the admission process seems to be more selective each year, and what was a given five years ago is no longer true." This means that students who may have had the impression as freshman that earning the valedictorian or salutatorian title would make them a shoo-in for a top school may have been misdirecting their efforts.

If my GPA doesn't guarantee me a spot, then what does?

Counselor Teresa Knirck says that unlike in the past, "the transcript is now the determining factor, not the GPA." When applying to college, students who are ranked at the top of their class should carefully consider what will happen when they are among all the other valedictorians and salutatorians. Director of counseling services Carol A. London says that every valedictorian and salutatorian should know that he or she is "not a shoo-in at the most academically-rigorous colleges. The student needs to know him or herself well enough to know if they are satisfied with not being number one in an institution." Remember, someone will always be at the bottom of the class, even at Harvard and Yale.

A few counselors even acknowledge that some students who vie for the number one spot in their class are engaged more in competition than actual learning. Counselor Bruce A. Smith says, "Our school's valedictorians and salutatorians are not necessarily our best students. GPA is a narrow measure of ability. The Ivy Leagues have thousands of valedictorians and salutatorians apply." Educational consultant Suzanne Luce notes, "Colleges do not want students that will just sit in their dorm room and study. They need to be interesting and involved." Suzanne F. Scott, a certified educational planner, says that students with very high GPAs "should apply early where there is rolling admissions. They should maximize their high school opportunities for their own personal growth, rather than try to package themselves with what they perceive colleges want."

FROM THE COUNSELORS

"No one is a shoo-in for a top college. The most competitive colleges are reaches for every student. Wellness is critical for students: Work diligently on academics, pursue at least one interest you love, get enough sleep, and enjoy your high school years."

–Shirley Bloomquist
Independent college counselor
A Second Opinion

"Students need the whole package. There are [approximately] 56,000 vals and sals, but many fewer total slots at the most selective colleges."

–Scott White
Director of guidance
Montclair High School

But isn't getting in the most important thing?

Of course, many valedictorians and salutatorians have achieved academic excellence not because they are nerds or bookworms, nor because they have attempted to manipulate the grading system to create a false image of themselves, but because they are brilliant young people who have the intelligence, determination, and desire to learn what is necessary not only to succeed in school, but also to achieve great things with their lives. Independent counselor William Morse says, "One easily finds lists of Nobel winners, and other men and women of achievement, who did not get in to this or that college. College does not make the man or woman. You, not some name college, determine your future achievements. Passion, discipline, and drive are key. Pursue top academic achievement along with at most one or two outside activities that mean the most to you. This is not about grades or balance; it is about depth and genuine commitment."

"Often, our top students overload themselves with activities and leadership responsibilities. Students need a balanced academic and extracurricular life and time to lay on the grass, look at the clouds, and contemplate life!"

–Sheila Nussbaum
School counselor
Hall High School

GRADES VS. CLASS RANK

Which matters more to colleges?

Norah, junior, New Jersey, got a great score on the ACT, is in the top 5% of her class, and has all A's, and she wants to get into an Ivy League school

---

So what's better—a high GPA or a high class rank? Ideally, you'd be hitting stratospheric levels in both (they do usually go hand in hand). But when the chips are down, what matters more?

This is a complicated question because college admissions counselors have a really tough job: they have to compare thousands of students from different high schools against each other. There's no standard way for them to measure the value of grades or class rank because grading and ranking systems differ by school. In terms of GPA, many schools give extra grade points for Advanced Placement, International Baccalaureate, and other challenging classes. However, this isn't always the case, and some schools don't even offer these classes. In terms of rank, students at some schools can only be ranked highly if they take lots of difficult classes—but at some schools, it's entirely possible to be ranked high without even taking college prep courses. And some schools

FROM THE COUNSELORS

"Grades are most important. Balancing rigorous classes with a strong GPA is outstanding in the eyes of admissions officers. However, rank puts your GPA in context. It offers insight as to the school you come from, your classmates, and how your GPA stacks up against others in your class."

–Keri Miller
School counselor
Minnetonka High School

are smaller and less difficult than others—so a student who's ranked 1 out of 40 at a school that's not very demanding might not be as strong as a student who's ranked 100 out of 500 at a top-tier high school.

So what do college counselors think? Do grades or rank matter more? According to most of the counselors we surveyed, grades are the most important criteria used by admissions officers. They feel, however, that class rank does matter quite a bit as well. On the other hand, some counselors disagree with the majority and feel that class rank is more important, and others feel the two are ranked equally. You could say there is a range of opinion when it comes to this subject.

Does it matter what classes these good grades are in?

Most counselors emphasize the importance of grades—and, in particular, grades in challenging classes. "Grades are weighted more heavily than class rank, and particularly so if the course is an accelerated, honors, IB, or AP course," argues consultant Lindy Kahn. "These classes are viewed as challenging the student, and colleges weigh that factor considerably." Counselor Keri Miller agrees. "Grades are most important," says Miller. "Balancing rigorous classes with a strong GPA is outstanding in the eyes of admissions officers."

Admissions officers are quite aware that a student can have an inflated rank by taking easy classes, so they definitely want to see evidence of success in academically-rigorous classes. In fact, as counselor Marie Soderstrom reports, "Many college applications ask counselors to rate the level of difficulty of courses taken by students compared to their fellow students." This also accounts for the fact that some teachers are more challenging than others. In other words, if you got a B in physics from the teacher who almost never gives

"I don't think there is one answer to this question. There's no getting around the fact, however, that being number one in your class does mean something."

–Lynda McGee
College counselor
Downtown Magnets High School

A's, and your friend got an A from the easy physics teacher, your counselor will have the opportunity to put your B in context.

What if my school doesn't rank students?

Furthermore, as a number of counselors pointed out, grades are more important than ever because many schools aren't ranking their students anymore. "Since many schools nowadays don't rank, grades are a universal currency of quality," explains consultant Lloyd R. Paradiso. That said, while most counselors argue that grades are more important than class rank, there are some with a differing opinion. "Since grades can be inflated, class rank appears more significant," argues counselor Leonora Saulino. And as counselor Lynda McGee points out, "There's no getting around the fact that being number one in your class does mean something."

However, some counselors argue that neither grades nor rank are more important—and that they're too closely related to be counted as entirely different measurements. As counselor Molly Tait puts it, "I think grades and rank complement one another." Moreover, counselor Keri Miller explains, "Rank puts your GPA in context. It offers insight as to the school you come from, your classmates, and how your GPA stacks up against others in your class."

Just as rank provides an important context for GPA, grades are the most important part of class rank. "Without the grades, you don't have a high class rank," points out counselor Marie Soderstrom. So does this mean that grades are more important than class rank, but that class rank matters too? Maybe, but it's important to remember that when a college admissions officer picks up your application, you really can't know for sure exactly what's going to be most important. Consultant Lloyd R. Paradiso believes that the question of grades versus rank is too general of a question because the admissions process is not the least bit uniform. As a student, concentrate on what you can control: getting grades that are as high as possible in the most challenging classes available, which will likely lead to a high class rank and an impressed admissions officer.

SAT SCORE VS. AP CLASSES

Which one matters more when applying to college?

Chloe, sophomore, Maine, is in all honors classes, and she is hoping for a scholarship to go to school somewhere in California

Tired of taking all of those high school exams? Sorry, it's not over yet—at least not if you plan to go to college! To make matters worse, you may have to do more than just take the SATs or ACTs. To be truly competitive, many students also take SAT Subject Tests or Advanced Placement tests. So what do college admissions officers prefer—students who aced an Advanced Placement test or students who aced an SAT Subject Test? And what the heck are these things anyway?

Are the tests really that different?
First off, here's what you need to know about these two kinds of tests—and what makes them different. Advanced Placement tests are administered at the end of Advanced Placement classes, which are a series of advanced level high school classes approved by the College Board that are designed to mimic the difficulty level of college courses. These optional AP tests (which are not required even if a student takes an AP course, though necessary to take if a student wants to get college credit) are a combination of multiple choice and essay. The tests are graded on a scale from 1 (the lowest score) to 5 (the highest). Almost all colleges and universities in the United States award students college credit if they score at least a 4 on the exam. Many schools also award credit for a score of 3.

What about SAT Subject Tests?
SAT Subject Tests are open to all students regardless of what classes they take. These multiple choice tests do not earn students college credit. However, selective schools require students to take between two and five SAT Subject Tests.

So, doesn't this mean the tests are very different? Yes and no. On the one hand, the official purpose of these tests is different. As guidance counselor and director Lester Eggleston, Jr., explains, "SAT Subject tests are used for admissions purposes. AP tests are used for placement once admitted." Furthermore, as educational consultant Jody Zodda points out, SAT Subject Tests are only required by the most selective schools—while virtually all colleges and universities in the United States accept AP credit.

On the other hand, both SAT Subject Tests and AP tests can be used as supplemental information on a student's application. Success on an AP test or an SAT Subject test—as well as success in an AP class itself—all provide data to a college about a student's willingness and ability to take on rigorous course work.

Furthermore, although most colleges do not require SAT Subject Tests, they will look at the scores and consider them as supplemental data. In this way, SAT Subject Tests can serve the same purpose as the AP test in the eyes of the admissions office—additional information about your academic abilities. And, as educational consultant Leslie Kent points out, "Some students, particularly those in small or rural schools, may not have access to AP courses because the school doesn't offer them." For these students, the SAT Subject Test can provide students the opportunity to demonstrate proficiency in a topic, even though an AP class isn't available.

So, do colleges prefer one of these tests over another?
This depends on who you ask. Many guidance counselors and other educational experts claim that schools treat the tests equally. As guidance counselor Kathy Boyd argues, "I don't know if college admissions officers prefer one

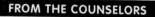

FROM THE COUNSELORS

"The AP and SAT are apples and oranges. Subject Tests are used in the admissions process at some colleges. AP scores are used for credit and/or placement once a student enrolls."

–Laura Barber
Director of guidance
Somers High School

over the other, but I would assume it doesn't matter much and that they both send a clear message of subject understanding."

However, other experts believe schools do a have a preference for one test or the other. According to educational consultant Keith Berman, admissions officers see the SAT Subject Test as a better measure of a student's ability to succeed in the college environment. "AP exams, and the scores, are a representation of a different ability: the ability to meet the high school's expectations," argues Berman. "SAT Subject Tests reflect your ability to identify courses that are appropriate, and to study independently. In this way, SAT Subject Tests are much more important, as the skill required to prepare for them is akin to studying for, say, a college midterm. The admissions office is, very roughly speaking, trying to ascertain your ability to thrive in college, so Subject Tests matter more."

On the other hand, some experts argue that admissions officers appreciate the rigor demonstrated by success on an AP test. Jon Reider argues, "APs are more sophisticated and based on a deeper level of knowledge, so they say more about how much a student knows relative to a very able peer group of test takers."

Any other advantages of one over the other?

Furthermore, as many experts point out, AP tests offer one distinct advantage over the SAT—namely, the time and money a student can save by earning college credit after passing an AP test. In addition, many high schools weigh grades in AP classes higher than in other classes, so a student's overall GPA can be bolstered by AP participation.

"This is how they are different: AP exams, and the scores, are a representation of a different ability, the ability to meet the high school's expectations. SAT Subject Tests reflect your ability to identify courses that are appropriate, and to study independently. In this way, SAT Subject Tests are much more important, as the skill required to prepare for them is akin to studying for, say, a college midterm."

–Keith Berman
Certified educational planner
Options for College
and Rudolph Steiner School

"APs are more sophisticated and based on a deeper level of knowledge, so they say more about how much a student knows relative to a very able peer group of test takers."

–Jon Reider
Director of college counseling
San Francisco University High School

So which test should you take? If both are an option, of course, this can't hurt. But if you only plan to take one, it really depends on your situation. If you're applying to elite schools, you'll probably have to take the Subject Test. If AP classes are not offered at your school, you may choose to take the subject test for this reason. If both options are available, talk to your guidance counselor to help determine the best possible strategy for your situation.

AP-PLY YOURSELF

How many AP courses should I take if I want to apply to selective schools?

Jasmine, junior, Pennsylvania, is feeling a bit overwhelmed taking five AP classes, but she is hoping to get into Princeton

If you want to attend elite schools, the courses you take in high school can matter quite a bit (no surprise there). Selective schools expect that prospective students will take and do well in Advanced Placement classes. But how many Advanced Placement classes does a student with elite college aspirations need to take?

Guidance counselors and other educational experts tend to fall into two camps surrounding this question. On one hand, some experts feel that in order to be competitive, students really need to take as many AP classes as they possibly can. On the other hand, counselors argue that although AP courses are important, it's equally important not to overdo it, especially since taking too many challenging classes at once can significantly impact your GPA or your ability to participate in extracurricular activities that enhance your college application.

Some experts feel that to be competitive, students must load up on AP classes and take "as many as humanly possible," as guidance counselor Eleanor Kinsella puts it. Educational consultant Keith Berman agrees, arguing that admissions offices at elite schools see AP classes as important evidence of educational rigor and excellence. "For better or for worse, AP courses usually represent the type of high school class where a student will be challenged, and end up at a new level of understanding by the end," he says.

But is there a minimum number of AP classes?
So, other than "as many as humanly possible," do these experts feel that there is a specific number of AP classes a student should take? For elite school admissions, some experts feel that four or five total classes throughout your entire high school education is the bare minimum you should take. "In your most

selective schools, I would think at least six," says educational consultant Judy Zodda. "That and good SAT scores are just the baseline." Counselor Karen Brodsky agrees. "We counsel students to take as many AP classes as they are capable of," she says. "Some take five or six a year." On the other hand, educational consultant Leslie Kent argues that there's no "magic number" when it comes to AP courses. "It depends on what's available and what you plan to study in college," says Kent.

And don't I get college credits?

In addition, along with the issue of college admission, a heavy load of AP classes comes with another tangible advantage—college credits. Although college credits are not guaranteed when a student takes an AP class, these classes give students the opportunity to take Advanced Placement tests and earn college credits. Considering the cost of elite educational institutions, credits earned in high school can be monetarily valuable. (Seriously, there was a girl in one graduating class whose entire undergraduate education only lasted two years thanks to all the AP credits she earned.)

However, not all guidance counselors and educational experts feel that it's important to load up on AP classes—even if you intend to apply to elite schools. While experts agree that a fairly heavy load of AP classes is important for admission, others feel that it's possible to take too many AP classes.

What if I don't think I can handle that many?

Most importantly, students need to be careful not to take more AP classes than they can handle—otherwise they risk seriously damaging their GPAs. But other counselors also emphasize the importance of maintaining a balance

FROM THE COUNSELORS

"[Students should take] as many AP courses as they possibly can. Highly selective schools will have far more qualified applicants than they can admit. What sets accepted students apart? First and foremost, drive. Drive expresses itself in many ways, the most quantifiable of which is how strenuously they challenge themselves in their high school education."

–Katie Small
College counselor
The Princeton Review

"[Students should take] as many AP classes as they are capable of taking without over extending themselves or driving themselves and everyone else nuts. Making this judgment on the number of AP courses that are reasonable requires some maturity and guidance from school staff, more than it does from the parents."

–Jim Prag
College counselor
Chaminade College Preparatory School

between academic achievements and keeping stress levels in check. "I don't think that it's necessary for a student to take three or four APs their senior year and be so stressed with their work that they can hardly function," says educational consultant Kiersten A. Murphy. "I want my students to be healthy. I would imagine that colleges want healthy students who are also contributors to the community around them." Educational planner Jodi Robinovitz agrees. "Being happy, healthy, and well adjusted and going to a less selective college is far more important than being overly stressed out by trying to win admission to one of the top-tier colleges," she states.

Other experts argue that students should focus primarily on taking AP classes that are relevant to their proposed field of study. "It might be ok for the future engineer to skip AP English or the student interested in journalism to skip AP Physics," argues Leslie Kent. Excessive time spent in an AP class that does not match a student's talents or interests may detract from time spent in an AP class the student really needs to ace.

So how many AP classes do you need? Clearly, AP courses are an important part of an application to an elite school. If you can take "as many as humanly possible" and do well in them, you're bound to impress a college admissions office (not to mention your bank account thanks to the courses you can skip in college). However, if a schedule full of AP courses is going to negatively impact your GPA—and your mental health—consider cutting back, at least a little bit.

"A student should take AP courses in the areas in which they have an interest and a passion and wish to be challenged to learn the material. But a student should not be taking APs just to take APs."

–Barbara W. Le Winter
President
Making the Grade to College, LLC

GRADE INFLATION

Is a B in an AP class better than an A in a regular class?

Arianna, sophomore, Texas, is in the top 5% of her class, and she plans on going to school for pre-med

This is an interesting philosophical question, and many of our respondents felt so strongly about it that they gave one-word answers: yes. Or, as counselor Jane Mathias put it: "Yes, yes, yes!" The overwhelming consensus is that students are better off taking Advanced Placement classes because colleges appreciate the effort of taking on a challenge when a student could easily have taken a less-strenuous course in the same subject. And if that means getting a somewhat lower grade, the sacrifice will be worth it. Not to mention having a chance at turning that class into college credit.

Many high schools weigh AP grades more heavily so that students aren't punished for taking on the more rigorous class. In other words, a B in the AP class usually is tabulated the same as an A in the less challenging class. "The GPA is the same, but the AP gives the student a more challenging course," says

FROM THE COUNSELORS

"I like the B in the AP class. You have a good grade, and the AP class is far more rigorous than the regular prep class. No C in AP classes, however."

—Cynthia Martini
College counselor
CHM College Advising Service

Jennifer Tabbush, president of Headed for College. "The stronger schedule always looks better," adds counselor Jeannette Adkins.

Many respondents agreed with certified education planner Jamie Dickenson's assessment that the "difficulty of the curriculum" in AP courses is "extremely important" to college admissions officials. "I think rigor is more important than the grade," adds Janice M. Hobart, CEO of College Found. "We are told that is what they look at first."

"There's a big difference between an A and a B," admits Glenn Ribotsky, a master tutor for The Princeton Review, "but a 92 in an AP course may be looked upon favorably compared to a 95 in a regular course." That said, not everyone agrees with this line of thought. In response to the question, Harriet Gershman, a certified education planner with Academic Counseling Services Inc., said simply: "Not always." "It depends on the school," adds Kathleen B. Grant, dean of students at Catlin Gabel School in Portland, Oregon. "But in general, they say the lower grade in a higher level course is better. I'm a little mixed about whether this is true at all schools."

"When asked, [colleges] will usually say, 'Take the AP course and get an A,'" says educational consultant Pearl Glassman, pointing out the paradox of admissions standards that can leave high schoolers scratching their heads as they contemplate what classes to take, and how difficult they should be, during senior year. Heather Britton-Doucette, a counselor at John Stark Regional High School in Weare, N.H., says she always advises her students to take "a more challenging class," because GPA isn't always the most important factor. But she acknowledges that she's "starting to wonder if that is the right advice, when I look at [some schools'] admissions records."

"I think admissions officers would like to see some AP classes, even if it means getting a B rather than an A. Selective colleges are hesitant about students with all A's, none of which have been earned in advanced classes. They question why such a good student would not challenge themselves."

–Joette Krupa
Director
College Placement Consultants

What if I'm not sure I'll make a good grade in an AP class?

If you have the chance to take an AP class, go for it. It's not a knock against the teacher or classmates you would have had in the "regular" class, but being in AP will give you more freedom to speak up and exchange ideas about the subject. A good teacher will encourage robust debate and discussion, just like in a college seminar, and soon the class will feel like a close-knit salon. You'll feel elevated, and a bit more prepared for college. Getting to skip an introductory math class or English comp in college is a bonus that you'll be thankful for in the fall of your freshman year. Your parents will be overjoyed as well, especially if they're footing the bill. According to the Texas Education Agency, some families have saved as much as $18,000 in tuition and expenses for credit accumulated on AP exams.

Just being in an AP class doesn't excuse you from putting in some serious work. There's no shame in getting a B, but anything below that, our counselors warn, might hurt you on the college app. Ms. Mathias, the counselor who said "Yes! Yes! Yes!" in response to our question, immediately followed that sentiment with this cautionary note: "But do not let it slip to a C." To avoid this, Mathias says, students should seek out extra help from any source they can, such as supplementary instruction books.

SAT VS. ACT

Which test is right for me?

Emerson, junior, Iowa, is a C student who has recently decided to work harder for better grades, because he doesn't want to wind up going to a community college before transferring to a university

Standardize tests: love 'em or hate 'em, they're one more way colleges and universities have to find out more about you and to make comparisons among qualified applicants. The SAT and the ACT are the two big ones, and they differ a bit in style, in emphasis, and in how students and counselors see them. Which one is the best choice for you? There are ways to investigate that. Read on.

"Our local university, University of Alaska—Fairbanks, prefers the ACT, but will accept SAT scores as well. I recommend that students read the admissions material from their schools to decide whether or not to take both tests," says counselor Mary Kovis Watson. You'll want to find out if the schools you are considering require or prefer one over the other, and a little digging, or outright asking admissions officials, will also tell you which one most students applying to a particular college take. Also, if you are applying for freshman admission to a specialized program, such as one in engineering, architecture, or the arts, you'll want to make sure to read what your department or school says, as well as general guidelines for admission to the university.

Are they really that different?

You're also going to want to think about what your strengths are in taking tests, and research the tests themselves to learn more about what they are like. "Neither is better—but one might be better for the student depending on which one they find more suited to their test-taking needs and inclinations," points out director of college counseling Barbara Simmons. "I have many students try both tests," adds independent counselor Ronna Morrison. "Just knowing that options exist reduces the pressure." Both testing companies offer practice tests, which you may want to consider taking. "We actual-ally have our students look at the PLAN and the PSAT which they take in the 10th and 11th grade to see which type of test suits them best," says Barbara Simmons. "Some test companies also have a practice ACT/SAT test which helps our students decide." You can also find informal practice tests online, not to mention in books that contain sample tests (**Cracking the SAT** and **Cracking the ACT** come immediately to mind), and there are courses which teach test strategies, such as those offered by The Princeton Review and other companies, as well.

Should I take both?

"Students should take one of each to see which test they do better on," advises counselor Gregory Rico. "Once they know which one better suits their learning and test taking ability they should prep for that test in the manner that best matches their learning style." "If students are not happy with their initial scores on either exam, I encourage them to try a practice exam of the other type under exam conditions to see if they do better on one," says Educational Options director Renee L. Goldberg. In educational consultant Nancy P. Masland's experience, "The SAT is best for those who test well, while the ACT is best for serious overachievers—often I suggest both."

In the end, it comes down to a matter of your personal style with standardized tests, how that relates to the test itself, how prepared you are, and sometimes, as with any other test you've taken in your school life, just how well things go on test day. It's wise to give yourself time to research the tests, time to prepare, time to take both tests (if that's what you want to do), and to take them more than once if you aren't happy with your scores. Each test is administered six or seven times a year and you can find out where local testing centers are from your counselors or by researching online. Ultimately, it's about giving

FROM THE COUNSELORS

"I formerly worked as a college admissions officer and we always gave the applicant the benefit of the doubt—meaning we used the higher score from whichever test when considering their file."

—Sarah Soule
Director of college counseling
Vermont Commons School

"Neither is better—but one might be better for the student depending on which one they find more suited to their test-taking needs and inclinations. Most colleges do not prefer one over the other."

—Barbara Simmons
Director of college counseling
Notre Dame High School

yourself your best shot to do well. "Take each test once, then concentrate on redoing the one you get the highest score on. I take colleges at their word that they treat the two tests the same," says college advisor Helene Kunkel.

"I recommend that students read the admissions material from their schools to decide whether or not to take both tests."

–Mary Kovis Watson
Counselor and teacher
Career Education Center–Fairbanks

"I encourage students to take both tests, because they may do exceptionally better on one over the other. I don't think any of the colleges care which one a student takes."

–Kate McVey
Director of college advising
Brebeuf Jesuit Preparatory School

TAKE ONE, TAKE TWO, TAKE THREE...

How many times should I take and retake standardized tests?

Isabel, senior, Oregon, has taken the SAT twice and is considering signing up for a test-prep course, and she is undecided about where to go to school and what to study

The most important tests required for college admissions are either the SAT or the ACT. Nearly all colleges will accept either one, but taking at least one of them is most often mandatory. But how do you choose which one to take and retake? Independent counselor Tracy Spann says, " I recommend that students take both the ACT and SAT once, then repeat the test on which they have scored the highest. I strongly suggest that students practice between test dates, to review skills that may have been taught in earlier high school years and then forgotten." There is a misconception that certain schools, especially on the East Coast, favor the SAT. However, this is simply no longer true. Counselor Sheila Nussbaum addresses this. She tells her students, "Choose the test prep method that best suits your learning style and schedule...Consider taking the ACT as well. It works better for some students."

How many times you take the tests depends, of course, on what score you get and what the average score ranges are for students accepted into the colleges you're interested in. But counselors agree that you should take either the SAT or the ACT in your junior year. Co-director of college counseling Letitia W. Peterson says, "Try to test by mid-year junior year with some general preparation and then fine-tune any areas that need improving with more focused preparation." This will allow for another testing opportunity during the senior year, if necessary. Independent counselor Trey Chappell tells his students, "Start testing mid way through junior year—take both the SAT and ACT, then retest only on whichever test you score higher on. This timeline gives students enough room to both retest and to sit for SAT Subject Tests, if they need to."

What about those practice tests I took sophomore year?

Another way to tell whether you should take the SAT or the ACT is to take the PSAT or the PLAN. The PSAT is a practice SAT, and the PLAN is a practice ACT. Both of these tests are available to sophomores and juniors, and they help students to get an idea of what their score would be on the real SAT or ACT. Not only will taking both these tests (if they are available in your area) help you to know which test you will perform better on, but also you will gain the valuable experience of taking a formally proctored exam in a realistic testing environment, without the worry of scores going onto your permanent record. PSAT and PLAN scores are never released to colleges. Counselor Scott Fisch tells his students to "always take the PSAT [or PLAN] to learn about time management."

The timeline for taking the standardized tests required for admission to four-year colleges and universities is a path fraught with anxiety for many students and their parents. With the alphabet soup of the PSAT, PLAN, ACT, SAT, and SAT Subject Tests, knowing which tests to take, when to take them, and how to prepare can be rather confusing. But college counselors agree on a basic timeline that will work for most students.

How do I make a studying timeline?

Once you have determined which test to take, you have to decide how best to prepare. Independent counselor Valerie Broughton explains her test prep philosophy this way: "I advise students to prepare in earnest for their ACT or SAT, take a course or use a book, start two months ahead of time, and get help. In an ideal world, I believe students could take the test only once. The tests are designed to be reliable. That means that you'll likely score in the same range every time you take it—unless you do something intentional to improve your score. The intentional action students can take is to prepare. So, why not prepare before the first sitting?"

For freshmen and sophomores who still have a while before having to take the tests, a long-term approach to test preparation could be useful. Counselor Tracie Morrison offers this advice: "Read. Read. Read. I was previously an English teacher and one of the strategies I instituted in my class was Silent Sustained Reading for about 20 minutes. Students can read whatever they want, but it must be quiet and it must be for 20 minutes. Having proctored the SAT, I notice that is the one area where students tend to struggle the most."

Anything else I can do?

Other methods of preparation are also available. Counselor Bruce A. Smith tells his students "Taking a timed practice test will help you with pacing. Plus, [when it's time to take the actual test] you'll understand the directions and won't have to spend as much time on directions during the test." Independent counselor Sandra Bramwell-Riley advises, "Read a wide cross-section of scholarly magazines. Invest in a number of SAT [or ACT] books, three at the most, and do them all."

What about prep courses?

There are also professional test preparation courses available to provide students with guided practice and techniques to improve their test scores. Carol A. London, a director of counseling services says, "We recommend that a student take the SAT or ACT three times: two times in the junior year and one time in the senior year. If the score is not what the student wants or needs, we recommend that he or she take a course to improve their test-taking skills."

FROM THE COUNSELORS

"Look at the results of the PSAT [or PLAN] to gauge what preparation is advisable. Take the tests in the winter of junior year to help predict which range of colleges might be best to visit over spring break, and to allow time to retake them in late spring."

–Letitia W. Peterson
Co-director of college counseling
Holton-Arms School

"I believe strongly in test preparation. I also believe that too many attempts make the students so nervous they cannot perform at all."

–Susan Hanflik
Educational consultant

And what about SAT Subject Tests?

The SAT Subject Tests are required for many of the more competitive colleges and universities, including all University of California schools. Which tests may be required vary from one college to the next, so check with your counselor or the school's website to make sure you're taking the right one or ones. Suzanne F. Scott, a certified educational planner, says, "Students should be advised to take SAT Subject Tests just after completion of certain courses, e.g., chemistry."

In the end, testing is just one part of the application, and though test scores are important, they shouldn't be focused on too heavily. As independent educational consultant Sue Bigg reminds her students, "Remember: Courses and grades are more important than test scores."

"Take a practice test or two from one of the readily available test guidebooks. Get a good night's rest the night before. Have a great breakfast the morning of the test. Dress for the test as if you were going to church or a nice restaurant. How you feel will impact how well you approach the test."

–Bill Kellerman
Educational consultant
College 101

LEARNING CURVE

What are the options for students with learning disabilities?

Charlotte, senior, Indiana, has a certification to take standard-ized tests un-timed because of a learning disability, and she wants to go to school for journalism

If you're a student with a learning disability, the key here is allowing plenty of time—months, in fact—to fill out the proper paperwork and have it approved by the College Board (which oversees tests like the SAT, PSAT, and AP cours-es) or ACT (www.act.org). Those who need accommodations for tests, such as extra time, large-print materials, or a person to read questions to you, will find themselves entering a bureaucratic maze apart from the testing process itself. But rest assured that your guidance counselor is well-versed in the pro-tocols and deadlines (the vast majority who responded to our survey knew all the right acronyms and steps to take) the process entails. "We have an SSD coordinator who can discuss the necessary paperwork required for extended time with the SAT and ACT," says counselor Jan Freund. "We have a pre-refer-ral process that works perfectly at our school," adds counselor Beth Thayer.

FROM THE COUNSELORS

"There are many [options available to LD stu-dents]—extended time, large print, use of computer/keyboard to write essays—so stu-dents should talk early to the testing organi-zations (ACT or ETS) if any of these things are an issue and get the documentation together well in advance."

–Glenn Ribotsky
Master tutor and teacher
The Princeton Review

It's worth mentioning, too, that the College Board's Services for Students with Disabilities (SSD) wing at the home office in Princeton, NJ, has all the guidelines on its website at CollegeBoard.com. So does the Educational Testing Service (ETS), which devises testing and scoring systems and administers the SAT under contract from the College Board. The ETS website (www.ets.org) has a lot of helpful links and FAQs.

What are examples of learning disabilities or other limitations that would earn me the right to special accommodations for a test?

According to the College Board, they can include vision and hearing impairment, learning disabilities (like attention deficit/hyperactivity disorder), and certain mental, physical or psychiatric disorders. More than three million students in the U.S. receive special-education services under the federal Individuals with Disabilities Education Act, but testing accommodations must be made on an individual basis, which is what explains the incredibly long advance time needed to obtain permission.

"Many different options are available with documented LDs that are verified and supported by the high school," says Jennifer Tabbush, president of Headed for College. "I refer my students directly to the ACT and College Board websites for testing accommodations. It is important to start the accommodations process at least four months prior to testing, as the process takes time and sometimes we have to appeal."

Will any request be granted?

Indeed, simply requesting a special consideration doesn't mean it will be granted. "Full accommodations are determined by the information provided,

"Each college usually has an office of student services. Contact this office as part of your college search so that you know before you apply whether your particular needs will be met at a given school."

—Jane Mathias
Director of guidance
Nardin Academy

but most students receive only extra time and not full accommodations such as readers, computer usage, and large print," says Harriet Gershman, a certified educational planner with Academic Counseling Services.

What kinds of accommodations are there?

According to ETS, there are many ways test-takers can be accommodated if they have documented disabilities or special needs. In addition to extra time, large print and in-person readers, these include:

- Sign-language interpreters

- Customized color backgrounds for computer test-takers

- Braille and cassette versions of tests

- Extra rest breaks

- A large-block answer sheet

- A different venue for taking the test, or special lighting

Additionally, the ACT allows disabled test-takers up to 50 percent more time than usual, up to five hours, with breaks in between. You can also arrange, through the College Board, to take an annual test (like the AP exam) at a different time if you have a temporary disability like a broken arm. For more information, the College Board can be reached at (609) 771-7137, and ETS is at (866) 387-8602. ACT is at (319) 337-1000.

Often, the barriers disabled students face go far beyond simple technological remedies. "SAT does provide accommodations, but many Latin students do not take advantage of this because the tendency is to not make the disability obvious," says counselor Rosa Moreno.

Everyone wants students with disabilities, learning and otherwise, to be on equal footing with their peers when it comes to test-taking, and these days there's more incentive than ever to make every accommodation that's deserved. Kurt M. Landgraf, president and CEO of ETS, says the No Child Left Behind Act established a deadline of 2014 for states to improve the academic performance of students with disabilities, and, according to him, "[the states] better get started."

What about in classrooms?

"At the classroom level, many teachers still aren't getting the appropriate support," Landgraf writes on the ETS website. "In general education classes, only 62 percent of secondary school students with learning disabilities are taught by teachers who say they get information about their students' needs or abilities. Part of the solution," he says, "involves educating educators on what works best for these students. Testing agencies have responsibilities, too. That's why ETS changed the way we report the scores of students who are granted test accommodations because of a disability—a change that avoids labeling students."

So there you have it. If you have a learning disability, or even a temporary physical impairment due to a skateboard accident, don't be shy about going to your counselor and finding out what options are available to you.

THIS IS A TEST...PREP

What are the pros & cons of test prep courses?

John, junior, Virginia, needs a great score on his standardized tests to help strengthen his application because his grades aren't that strong, and he wanted a football scholarship at an SEC school but got injured

Most counselors feel that test prep classes are an efficient way to help students improve their scores—at least some of the time. Some experts feel that prep classes are more valuable than others. "I never advise students to study on their own," says independent consultant Lindy Kahn. "If they can afford it, I have them sign up for a course."

However, other experts are more wary of test prep classes, and emphasize that they're not for everybody. Many argue that these classes are of little value unless you are willing to do the work, take the class seriously, and practice at home. "The more expensive review courses are only as good as the amount of time the student is willing to put into them," explains head counselor Marie Soderstrom. "If students don't practice what they are taught in the course, then they will waste anywhere from $1,000 to $1,500."

FROM THE COUNSELORS

"The more expensive review courses are only as good as the amount of time the student is willing to put into them. If students don't practice what they are taught in the course, then they will waste anywhere from $1,000 to $1,500."

—Marie Soderstrom
Head counselor
Edmond Memorial High School

Other counselors feel that prep classes are superior to independent study, but only in some situations. Consultant Lloyd R. Paradiso only recommends prep courses for students who thrive in a classroom setting. Some experts, like counselor Margaret Lamb, only recommend prep courses to students "when their PSAT scores are low, or when they have a track record of doing poorly on larger tests or on standardized tests."

Similarly, counselor Martha Sharp recommends prep courses for students who lack the motivation to study independently. Counselor Kerri Miller points out the prep courses can be very helpful for students with learning disabilities. And although head counselor Marie Soderstrom isn't a big fan of prep classes, she does feel they can be helpful for students who need a refresher course in algebra and geometry.

In addition, as dean of academic life Anne Weeks argues, prep courses can be helpful because they can build a student's confidence. "If they need to have their confidence built by exposure to the test and learning test taking skills, a test prep course can be worth it," she argues.

What if I can't afford a prep class?

On the other hand, many experts feel that the cheaper options—books, software, websites, and other inexpensive tools that offer practice tests and help students prepare—are just as good for some students. For students who are shy and uncomfortable in classroom settings, independent study can be a better option.

Consultant Rachel Winston recommends independent study for students who are very good at organizing their time. "Studying independently is only

"There are plenty of opportunities for kids to prepare for standardized tests that do not cost a fortune (or anything for that matter). If students are innately shy and non-participatory by nature in the classroom, I suggest private work or online assistance. If they thrive in a classroom situation, then I'll propose a group session. When finances are an issue, I will recommend the library and a ton of self-help. Occasionally, test prep firms will offer courses to the demonstrated needy at a reduced fee. When the need is legitimate, I urge these kids to ask."

–Lloyd R. Paradiso
President and CEO
The Admissions Authority

successful for those people who are very organized and able to focus," she explains. "This tends to include student-athletes whose time is very limited. Their tournament or competition schedule varies, so a weekly class schedule is not appropriate. These students have learned that to get anything done, they need to create their own study plan. For these students, independent studying is appropriate."

Are there any other options?

Because there are so many inexpensive alternatives to prep classes, students who cannot afford these classes still have many options. "For students who cannot afford a prep course, I advise them to seek materials from the library or local bookstore," says counselor Kerri Miller. Guidance director Margaret King mentions that "There are a few websites that do [test prep] for practically nothing."

Additionally, students who cannot afford expensive test prep courses with private companies may be able to find cheaper alternatives within the community. Counselor Leonora Saulino recommends that students look for test prep classes at local community colleges. Counselors sometimes can also get a hold of coupons to help students pay for test prep classes. And, as consultant Lloyd R. Paradiso points out, "Occasionally, test prep firms will offer courses to the demonstrated needy at a reduced fee. When the need is legitimate, I urge these kids to ask."

So are expensive prep classes worth the money? Yes, but not necessarily for all students. If you work better independently, or if you can't afford a class, independent study opportunities through print and web sources can help you quite a bit. And, as counselor Marie Soderstrom argues, it's important to keep in mind that outside test preparation isn't everything. "I am a firm believer that the curriculum a student takes throughout high school is the best test prep," she says.

DECLARE YOUR INDEPENDENCE?

Should I use an independent counselor?

Sophie, junior, Delaware, is a cheerleader and president of her class and of the honor society, and she wants to go to an Ivy League school

If you're a college-bound student with money to spend, it's easy to plunk down thousands of dollars on the college admissions process. From SAT prep courses to private tutors to cross-country college visits, the process can become quite expensive. But here's something many students don't know: if you want some extra help applying for colleges, you can hire an independent educational consultant to help you enhance your application.

What do these consultants do? For the most part, they do exactly what a good high school counselor does—only with more personal attention. They help students and parents identify appropriate colleges and offer advice on how to get admitted to these schools. In addition, they remind students and parents of deadlines, help families manage and complete the necessary paperwork, and give students advice on how to write application essays and create the best application possible.

Can't my high school guidance counselor help me with the admissions process?

Many high school guidance counselors cringe at the notion of an independent admissions consultant because they feel this service is a waste of money. They argue that this expensive service does nothing but duplicate what a high school guidance counselor can do for free. "I don't recommend independent counselors," says counselor Keri Miller. "I believe that school counselors are equipped with the same expertise.... You should never have to pay for college counseling." "We provide a wonderful free service to our students," argues counselor Marie Soderstrom. "College is expensive enough, so why add to that expense when they get counseling for free?" Counselor Leslie Munns agrees: "Why pay for what the school offers as a part of their mission?"

Other guidance counselors don't recommend independent counselors for one simple reason—they can't. This kind of service is more readily available in large urban areas (although this is changing, thanks to the Internet), so students from rural areas often don't have access to independent admissions consulting businesses.

Are there any advantages to independent counseling?

While many guidance counselors scoff at the idea of independent counseling, some begrudgingly admit that it can have its advantages. Because guidance counselor case loads are so heavy, an independent counselor may be able to give a student more individual attention—thereby freeing up a school counselor's heavy load a little. Counselor Mary Pat Anderson says she never recommends private counseling, but admits that "it makes my job easier," and that "students usually get good lists of schools."

Other guidance counselors emphasize the importance of families, school guidance counselors, and independent counselors all working together as a team. Educational consultant Marilyn Morrison agrees with this, noting that "Independent counselors do not take the place of high school counselors, but we can be a valuable supplemental resource."

Independent counselors feel they offer a valuable service to students and parents. Because college admission is becoming increasingly competitive, especially at the more selective schools, independent consulting can give students the advantage they need over their equally-qualified peers. In addition, applying to college is an arduous and confusing task, and consultants can help parents and students navigate their way through this process more easily.

FROM THE COUNSELORS

"I don't recommend independent counselors. I believe that school counselors are equipped with the same expertise. However, with large caseloads, it is important for students to seek out their school counselor. Make an appointment. Come with questions. Be prepared. You should never have to pay for college counseling."

—Keri Miller
School counselor
Minnetonka High School

Moreover, high school counselors are often overworked, and some students need more personal attention than their assigned counselor can give.

"I think we provide a valuable service to the public, for both self-motivated students and those that need more hand holding as well as a push in the right direction," says educational consultant Lindy Kahn. And when asked if he would recommend independent counseling to students, admissions consultant Lloyd R. Paradiso had this to say: "Of course! I am one! I recommend myself and my colleagues all the time. I also urge my friends in school positions to consider becoming independent when contemplating a career move." So there you have it—now it's up to you to decide if you need it.

How do you know if it's a scam?

Other counselors say they have no problem with independent counselors, but warn that students need to watch out for scams. As counselor Lynda McGee explains, "Most of my students can't afford independents, but if they could, I wouldn't have a problem with it as long as I knew they were worth it. I have had a few students sign up for those rip-off services where poor families pay $1,000 to have them fill out the FAFSA for them! Pitiful! I do that for free." Educational consultant Margaret King agrees. She warns parents and students to only do business with consultants who are members of the Independent Educational Consultants Association (IECA), the National Association of College Admissions Counseling (NACAC), or the Higher Educational Consultants Association (HECA).

"Considering that I am one, I think we provide a valuable service to the public, for both self-motivated students and those that need more hand holding as well as a push in the right direction."

—Lindy Kahn
Certified educational planner
Lindy Kahn Associates, Inc.

LEAD OR BE PART OF THE FLOCK

Should I diversify my application through extracurriculars and volunteering?

Christopher, sophomore, New Jersey, hasn't really been involved in extracurriculars but makes good (but not great) grades, and he wants an edge that will boost him from acceptable to preferred when applying to his reach school

Term papers, homework, chores—it can all be a bit overwhelming at times. But it still pays to make time for extracurricular activities and volunteer work. Believe it or not, this is also a big part of your education. Extracurricular activities such as sports, theater, or working on the school newspaper will broaden your interests and show that you're a team player. This trait is one of the intangibles that will be considered during your college application process, but it can go a long way in impressing the admissions office. As Dr. Dean P. Skarlis, president of The College Advisor of New York states, "Passion, leadership, and sincere interest in their activities trumps all else."

What do I pick?

When choosing the extracurricular activities, play to your strengths. Keep in mind that it's not just for fun and socializing; it can open doors for scoring some of those choice scholarships. Granted, not everyone will fill the

FROM THE COUNSELORS

"[I suggest] a leadership role in only one or two activities—the more focused and passionate a student [the more they] come across with greater commitment and interest. However, I have known a few students who actually try tons of things and are really good at all of them—but they are rare."

—Deborah Bernstein
Director of college counseling
Forest Ridge School of the Sacred Heart

quarterback's shoes and be handed a fully-funded football scholarship that leads straight to the NFL after graduation, but if you dig deep enough, there's something there for everybody.

That being said, there are a lot of sports scholarships that go unclaimed. Tech-related scholarships are particularly hot right now. If this is right up your alley, hook up with the computer club in your high school. If you're thinking of a future in business or civil service, check out the debate club. Language clubs (Spanish, French, Latin—sorry, Trekkies, no Klingon) are a great way to prepare for higher education. Why? Knowing another language goes a long way in expanding your vocabulary and spelling in your first language, along with impressing foreign border guards and snooty maître d's. As your study materials and text books get more complex and convoluted, knowing other tongues will help you understand the verbosity.

What about volunteering?

Volunteering also offers many benefits. If you have an idea of which direction you would like your higher education to take, choose a volunteer activity in that area. You'll gain real world experience (to complement all that dry, academic jibber-jabber) and know that you're working to improve your community. For these reasons, admissions officers hold volunteering in high regard. Donald Dunbar puts it this way: "Regardless of how good a student is, colleges favor kids who can add to their communities with a developed talent."

Volunteering is a great way to begin networking. Networking is incredibly important in today's workplace. Everybody's online and connected 24/7, meaning that many more people are working less as full-time employees than contract workers, brought in for a specialized issue and then free to leave once

"I believe that in-depth participation in two activities is better than superficial membership in many. I like at least one activity to be school-related. My advice is the same for students of all levels of ability and performance."

–Diane E. Epstein
Director
College Planning Service, Inc.

it's completed. When one assignment wraps up, another one must be found in close order to keep the cash flow going. Current statistics indicate that 30 percent of Americans are self-employed in one capacity or another, so to keep those greenbacks a-coming you're going to need a network of like-minded citizens.

Not all volunteering involves soup kitchens or picking up litter along the I-5. Thinking of being a veterinarian? The local animal shelter always needs a helping hand. Want to get some leadership experience on your résumé? Why not see about coaching in an after-school program or at a Boys & Girls Club?

Keep in mind that not all volunteer gigs are created equal, so it's good to know how much of a time commitment you're willing to make. Some are tightly focused; others, not so much. For example, people who organize 5K fun runs are always looking for volunteers. Do you like to be outdoors? This might be right for you. It only entails a few hours on Saturday morning. Nine times out of ten, the money goes to a deserving charity, so in the long run (pun intended) you'll be helping an enormous number of people while rubbing shoulders with people from all professions and walks of life (networking, again). Another couple of pay-offs are the free t-shirt and all the Gatorade you can stomach.

If a career in the medical profession is in your future, why not consider donating five or six hours a week at a hospital, clinic, or nursing home? Once you reach medical school, you'll have a good grasp of the concepts and terminology. On the other hand, through volunteering you might find that you're not a fan of the hospital scene and would rather go into botany.

Making time to engage in extracurricular activities and donating your time by volunteering can really give you the edge when you compete for that coveted spot at the campus of your choice. Spending your free time this way might leave your wallet a bit lighter than it would be if were flipping burgers, but it'll pay off in the future. The key to success is to develop a game plan now and stick to it.

GOING THE EXTRA MILE

Do colleges really care about extracurricular activities?

Zoe, sophomore, Washington, is in the band and maintains a B average, and she wants to go to school on the East Coast for music

When reviewing your application, college admissions officers are going to be first looking at your grades and what courses you took, along with perhaps your SAT and ACT scores. They'll also want to know what else you did with your time. Did you work after school? If so, what did you do? Were you even promoted while you were there? Did you play sports? Did you start a reading program in your community? Did you build sets for the theater department? Or maybe your time was taken up with caring for a sick parent or a younger brother? Colleges want to know all about how you spent your time both in and out of class so that they can get the clearest possible picture of who you are and where you are in your life. So it goes without saying that sometimes, how you spend your time outside the classroom can be just as revealing as how you fared academically. They are looking, among other things, to see what you've learned about leadership, teamwork, responsibility, and using your talents through the activities that you've engaged in.

How many should I do?

"Longevity and commitment to a few organizations, projects, or sports is much better than doing a lot of things for a very short time! This means a lot to college admissions reps," says Sarah Soule. Mary Kovis Watson adds, "I think the grades are the most important. Having one or two meaningful activities on an application can be very helpful, especially if the student really excelled at the activity." According to Renee L. Goldberg, extracurricular activities "have some influence, but in general, these activities are not as important as students think and hope." So what's the moral here? Extracurriculars can add sheen to a strong application, but if your grades aren't up to snuff, don't expect them to salvage your chances of acceptance.

Will my extracurriculars make up for my weaker grades?

"Extracurriculars matter, but only if everything else is in order," says Helen Kunkel. "Stellar extracurricular activities don't make up for so-so grades, low rigor of classes, and SAT's below the average for the schools you're looking at applying to." Barbara Simmons adds, "Extracurricular activities are important—probably not to the extent that an excess of them will carry a student into an acceptance, but to the extent that the student's involvement in activities beyond academic life shows breadth and energy."

"Athletics can play a large part in helping a borderline student gain admission at almost any college if the student has talent and the coach has an interest in bringing that talent to campus," says Rachel Elkins Thompson. But that's not something to count on, in sports or any other area. "Unless a student's participation has been outstanding (particularly in a sport), I believe extracurricular activities, work, and volunteering have less impact than students expect," says Ronna Morrison. Kate McVey agrees, noting, "I think it has some influence. The main factor is going to be the transcript. After that, the more selective a school is, the more these things matter. What is most important in this area is that the student is sincere about their participation."

What does it mean to be well-rounded?

Ultimately, interest, commitment, and passion are what extracurriculars come down to. It doesn't matter if your strongest point is ballet or football, teaching reading or working at the Burger Shack, so long as you make the most of your opportunities, and see how they fit in with your goals. And make sure the colleges see how that works for you: they will not be impressed by a long list of activities just for the sake of being able to put an activity on your application.

FROM THE COUNSELORS

"At the end of the process, if two students are equal academically, admissions will consider which student will bring more to the campus community."

—Carol Gill
President
Carol Gill Associates

"I think it has some influence. The main factor is going to be the transcript. After that, the more selective a school is, the more these things matter. What is most important in this area is that the student is sincere about their participation."

—Kate McVey
Director of college advising
Brebeuf Jesuit Preparatory School

"I would think that the colleges would want a well-rounded individual, one who would participate in their community," says Dr. Laurie H. Nash. And a well-rounded student is exactly what you want to present to colleges. Sports, a job, volunteering, family responsibilities—everything and anything that you do (within reason) will matter to the admissions office. "I think, while they show a student's breadth of interest and that the student has energies [that extend] beyond the classroom, they do not substitute for good grades and a rigorous course load," says Barbara Simmons. "They are probably not as important as students think." That said, they can make all the difference on a borderline application. Besides, it's better to put yourself out there than sit on the sidelines until it's too late.

"Extracurricular activities are important— probably not to the extent that an excess of them will carry a student into an acceptance, but to the extent that the student's involvement in activities beyond academic life shows breadth and energy."

—Barbara Simmons
Director of college counseling
Notre Dame High School

EXTRA-SPECIAL EXTRACURRICULARS

Are there certain extracurricular activities that admissions committees love?

Gianna, junior, California, has started her own clean-air-action non-profit, and she wants to study environmental science at University of California—Berkeley

"There is no one magical activity," says Jennifer Tabbush, president of Headed for College. "From debate to Model UN to pre-med club to music to community service, passion and commitment are what really matters." Indeed, much of the way colleges perceive your extracurricular interests depends on how you go about them—and your level of success in each one—rather than the interests themselves. Tabbush notes that admissions officers love to see students receive "national or state-level recognition" as well as positions of "increasing leadership" in student organizations. Similarly, counselor Heather Britton-Doucette notes that positions to which you're "elected or nominated by peers and faculty" can be boons to your admissions chances.

Should I just do a lot of different activities to be well-rounded?

As it's difficult to distinguish yourself if you continually hop from one interest to another, counselors recommend you choose activities that you think you'll

FROM THE COUNSELORS

"I am inclined to believe that leadership is highly valued, whether it involves being an Eagle Scout, president of the student body, editor of the yearbook, or even captain of the team. I also think students should volunteer—and not just once a year at a food bank. Most of all show some consistency in your activities. If you like something, stick with it and perhaps think of ways you can increase your involvement. For instance, if you love baseball, don't just play it—volunteer to teach or coach it, or be an umpire for little league games."

—Joette Krupa
Director
College Placement Consultants

want to stay with for a couple of years or more. And choosing activities that you like should make it easier to do well in them: "Whichever activities they choose, I think that students need to be genuinely interested in them," says educational consultant Pearl Glassman.

If you feel passionate about an interest for which there is currently no outlet in your area, organize something for it! Jane Mathias, director of guidance at Nardin Academy, states that admissions pros like to see "projects showing initiative rather than participation." You can start a cooking club, an organization that provides assistance to people who are homeless, or a group dedicated to the preservation of medieval musical instruments—whatever is important to you!

What if I don't really enjoy clubs and student government?

You can also opt to "do something 'outside of the box,'" says counselor Beth Thayer. Freida Gottsegen, a private college consultant, reports that such activities can, on occasion, "create a 'hook'" for admissions officers. A few years ago, CBS News reported on a high school student from Atlanta, Georgia who modified his diesel pickup truck to run mostly on vegetable oil. That summer he drove around the country telling people about fuel alternatives. He traveled 7,500 miles in his truck while spending only $5 on gasoline! Imagine the kind of interest that spurred at the admissions office.

Counselor Cynthia Martini says that if you initiate a unique activity, it will be viewed most positively if "it benefits others" in some way. Service-oriented activities are always popular with colleges, and the more traditional ones—like community service, student government, and tutoring—will certainly help you come admissions time if you show a real commitment to them.

"I find that colleges truly appreciate substantive school and/or community service. Two of our students founded the Natural Disaster Relief Fund in response to Hurricane Katrina. This group continues to function as a group that supports people who are victims of natural disasters. Colleges have been especially responsive."

–Hazel M. Shaw
College guidance counselor
James Madison High School

Aren't sports the best extracurricular since athletes get recruited for scholarships?

Sports—particularly "at a level where you are recruitable," says Jane Mathias—are other traditional activities that carry a lot of weight with admissions officers. "If a school is a powerhouse in lacrosse, then that student expertise is important," says Janice M. Hobart, CEO of College Found. If you're a goaltender and your prospective college's goalie is about to graduate, then you're even more valuable to that school!

Depending on what a college is looking for—and what the other students in its applicant pool bring to the table—your talents, experiences, or interests may fulfill one of its needs. Cynthia Martini adds that "Anything you do works if you are outstanding at it and they need it!"

BUCKS FOR JOCKS

How do I get recruited for athletic scholarships?

Brandon, junior, Georgia, is a pitcher for the baseball team,
which has a strong chance at the state championship this year,
and he wants to play for a Division I baseball team so he can get
to the Major League

So you're thinking your athletic prowess might pave the way to a college scholarship, but how do you go from hopeful athlete to collegiate superstar? "You need to be proactive," Counselor Cynthia Martini writes. Athletic scholarships are less common than their academic counterparts—Heather Britton-Doucette, guidance counselor at John Stark Regional High School, describes them as "few and far between"—and it can take an Olympic-sized effort to get noticed by the right college coaches.

When do I start the process?
That said, if you've had success in one or more sports, you should investigate whether your athletic ability can help defray the cost of your college education. This process usually begins late in your sophomore or early in your junior year, though it can start afterward if you're a late-bloomer on the playing field. It usually begins with what Jennifer Tabbush, president of Headed for College, describes as "a realistic assessment of your talent." For many students, this means "talking to their coach and getting his or her opinion about their qualifications for athletic scholarships," Pearl Glassman, educational consultant, writes. However, some situations may call for an outside opinion. "I am now working with a gymnast and we are consulting with a retired college gymnastics coach," Glassman notes. Once armed with an expert's assessment, and your own understanding of your talent, counselor Kathleen B. Grant advises you to "decide what division you want"—I, II, or III (there's a world of difference between each one!)—"and how much time you want to spend on sports."

What sorts of things can make me ineligible?
At this point, it's also a good idea to visit NCAAStudent.org, the NCAA's official website for prospective student athletes. Here you can download the Guide for the College-Bound Student Athlete, which includes a lot of useful in-

formation plus the NCAA's amateurism and academic eligibility requirements for playing at Division I and Division II schools. (Quick tip: If you already play for the Los Angeles Lakers, or have a GPA under 2.0, the NCAA will have serious concerns regarding your eligibility.) Students wishing to play at Division I or Division II schools register via NCAAClearingHouse.net (there's a registration fee, but it may be waived if you were granted a fee waiver for the SAT or ACT). Division III schools determine eligibility independently, though playing with Kobe or flunking your classes will raise red flags with them as well.

Can coach help me out?

Your current coach may have contacts at colleges and universities that offer your sport. If so, he or she can be an instrumental part of your search for funds. If not, don't worry—there's a lot you can do on your own. Yetunde Daniels Rubinstein, counselor at St. Peter's Prep, says a good starting point is "the on-line athlete-inquiry sheet available on most college websites." Summer athletic programs, usually held on college or university campuses, are great places to be spotted. If you can't make it to one—or even if you can—send a DVD of your competitions to coaches at schools you'd like to play for. A simple e-mail can also yield solid results. No matter what you do, follow up. It's important to remember that, depending on your current circumstances, coaches "may not be able to contact [you due to] NCAA rules," counselor Britton-Doucette writes. But you can "Let them know where they can see you play."

FROM THE COUNSELORS

"I tell [students] to showcase themselves if at all possible at summer camps, [and] to talk with their high school coaches about the level they should be looking at and if they have any college suggestions. They also should contact colleges and let them know they are interested in the school and tell the coaches they are interested in playing for them.

–Joette Krupa
Director
College Placement Consultants

Can my test grades help at all?

You should also take the PSAT. With this test under your belt, you'll be eligible for "official visits" to schools—expenses-paid trips where blue-chip recruits check out the campus, see games, and talk with coaches. Check out the NCAA's Guide for the College-Bound Student Athlete for more info on this.

What about verbal agreements?

Mere mortals, however, usually have to work for attention from coaches and schools. Jane Mathias, director of guidance at the Nardin Academy, warns about "mail merge" letters: Even when a school does reach out to you about your talent, your name may be coming from a very long list. And while verbal agreements between students and college coaches have become very popular, certified educational planner Harriet Gershman warns that "until you have that letter in hand"—specifically a National Letter of Intent, accompanied by a financial aid agreement—"nothing is final." Get it in writing!

"After counseling them on the infinite benefits of obtaining a college education with or without athletics, I have these students research athletic scholarships. We also put a Plan B in place, in case they do not receive a scholarship."

–Hazel M. Shaw
College guidance counselor
James Madison High School

LEND A HAND

How will volunteering or community service impact my college application?

Eric, sophomore, Arizona, volunteers with his church, and he wants to go to a state school that has a study-abroad option

A recent article in **The Onion**—a well-known satirical newspaper—"reported" that high school students were upset at the closing of a local homeless shelter because now they couldn't volunteer in order to pad their college applications. It's certainly a popular stereotype that students volunteer just to fatten up their applications, especially if they're applying to prestigious schools. But what's the reality? Do colleges really expect students to have community service on their college applications?

Some experts strongly feel that community service activities are needed to impress college admissions officers. "I believe a well-rounded student is viewed favorably by college admission officers," argues counselor Sara Irwin Goudreau. "A student who has the initiative to go out and willingly volunteer has the innate ability to go out and be accomplished in a multitude of areas." Guidance director Michael Dolphin agrees. "A well-rounded student impresses

FROM THE COUNSELORS

"I tell my students that the 'smorgasbord' approach is not what schools are looking for in students. They want dedicated involvement, and beginning this process can't happen the summer before the senior year. We begin this type of advisement with incoming freshmen. Disingenuous service is not going to help with the admissions process. The type of community service colleges are looking for is the type that truly impacts the community."

–Marie Soderstrom
Counselor

"It's another trumped up facet of the process to take attention away from what really counts and what lots of candidates don't possess: the best grades in the most challenging courses available in their school. Feeding the homeless will never be a substitute for the D in chemistry."

–Lloyd R. Paradiso
President and CEO
The Admissions Authority

college admission," he says. "Unselfishness in one's community is always looked upon favorably."

Consultant Rachel Winston argues that volunteerism is important because it demonstrates a student's passion and leadership abilities—two qualities that schools see as markers of an outstanding student. "This keen enthusiasm translates into a deeply committed student," she explains. "The choice of activity is not as important as whether or not they truly love the activity and give 100 percent to the effort."

Can I just help for a few hours and count that as volunteering?

Other experts argue that volunteer work can impress an admissions officer, but only if it comes across as genuine. Schools are on the lookout for application padding, and when they see it, they're not impressed. "Volunteering looks good only if it is consistent and true, not to pad the app," says counselor Margaret King. "Padding is very obvious to an admissions officer, and sometimes it has a negative effect."

As counselor Marie Soderstrom says, admissions officers are much more impressed with volunteerism that's part of a long commitment. "I tell my students that the 'smorgasbord' approach is not what schools are looking for in students," she explains. "They want dedicated involvement, and beginning this process can't happen the summer before the senior year. We begin this type of advisement with incoming freshmen. Disingenuous service is not going to help with the admissions process. The type of community service colleges are looking for is the type that truly impacts the community. For example, helping with a food drive once or twice is nice, but it won't cut it. Organizing and delivering annually, that is the real deal."

"Volunteerism, community service, leadership, and involvement are not necessary to gain admission to certain colleges. Larger state schools view these factors as secondary characteristics.... However, smaller colleges will take a look at these factors in making an admissions decision."

–Keri Miller
School counselor
Minnetonka High School

In addition, according to consultant Marilyn C. Morrison, schools like to see volunteer work that is consistent with other parts of the application. "Community service and volunteerism are most valuable when they are meaningful choices made by students that reflect their talents, interests, and goals," says Morrison. In other words, if you want to major in special education, volunteer as a tutor with learning disabled children. If you want to major in architecture, spend spring break building houses in New Orleans.

Is volunteering experience more important to private schools that to public ones?

"I'm not sure if it's necessary at all colleges, but an increasing number of [schools] are putting an emphasis on it—particularly the private schools," says counselor Margaret Lamb. "Many state schools are primarily numbers-driven." Counselor Keri Miller agrees, noting that "Larger state schools view these factors as secondary characteristics."

Is it really that helpful?

Although most counselors encourage community service and feel it can be at least somewhat helpful on an application, others argue that it isn't very important at all. "Admissions people do not communicate any excitement about seeing it on a transcript," claims counselor Leonora Saulino. Consultant Lloyd R. Paradiso agrees. Though he feels that a dedicated commitment to community service may look impressive, overall he thinks that volunteerism is too much about padding a student's college application. "It's another trumped-up facet of the process to take attention away from what really counts and what lots of candidates don't possess: the best grades in the most challenging courses available in their school," he says. "Feeding the homeless will never be a substitute for the D in chemistry."

Other counselors argue that volunteerism should not be a factor for admissions offices because this requirement is inherently elitist. "Many students have to work, and this should be taken into consideration," says Molly Tait.

So do you need volunteer work on you college applications? It probably can't hurt—unless it's obvious that you're padding your application—and many smaller, private schools do expect community service. However, not all community service activities look equally impressive. It's better to commit to a long-term project than a series of unrelated ones, and it's better to choose a project that reflects your future goals. So don't volunteer at that homeless shelter just to pad your application. However, if you feel it would be rewarding to make a long term commitment to working with the homeless, and if you plan to study a related major such as sociology or social work, this experience might look great on your application.

WORKING FOR THE WEEKEND

How does work experience influence a college admissions committee?

Pamela, senior, Arkansas, has a part-time job as a waitress and is saving for school because her grades are too low to hope for scholarships, and she wants to study communications at the University of Arkansas without going to community college first

You've heard it a million times: Colleges want to see lots of extracurricular activities on your application. But what if you can't get all that involved in extracurriculars because finances dictate that you work? And even if you don't have to work, or you don't work enough hours to prevent you from getting involved in activities, how does work look on a college application as compared to a full roster of extracurriculars?

Most of the experts surveyed here feel that work experience looks great on a college application—and that if you put your work experience in the right context, it can look just as good as extracurricular activities. The trick is to discuss what you've gained from your work experience and how it reflects your positive qualities—just as you would if you were writing about extracurriculars.

Consultant Joan Bress explains, "The question an admissions officer always asks is, 'What has the student done with what he or she has?' An after-school

FROM THE COUNSELORS

"I think work experience does influence college admission, in a positive way. I think that admissions officers take into account zip codes and the possible need for a student to work to pay their own expenses, or even help out with family expenses. I also think it demonstrates responsibility if you have a job. If you can find a job that relates to your interests, even better."

–Judy Zodda
Educational consultant
Zodda College Services

job offers as many opportunities to demonstrate leadership and initiative as an extracurricular activity. I advise students who work to set performance goals for themselves and to keep a record of their accomplishments. Some of the best essays I've read have been about work-related experiences." Counselor Jim Prag agrees, saying, "Let the college know how that job experience shaped you and your thinking—just like you would do with extracurriculars."

Does it matter if the job isn't related to my future career?

Other counselors add that if a job experience relates to a student's future plans, they can emphasize this in the application—just as a student can emphasize extracurricular activities that relate to future plans. As consultant Judi Robinovitz states, "Work is just another extracurricular activity—[but one that's] especially important for a future business major, among others!"

Other experts feel that students should play up their work experience because schools value work ethic and responsibility. "Work is terribly important," says consultant Barbara W. LeWinter. "It exposes kids to the real world and helps them recognize that they will encounter and need to work with all kinds of people." Counselor Kerri Durney agrees. "I think that employment is looked highly upon by college admission officers," she says.

What if I have to work so much I don't have time for extracurriculars?

Experts advise that students discuss this with pride on their applications, noting that students who have to take on economic responsibilities at an early age display character and work ethic. Admissions officers are plenty sick of students who have a strong sense of entitlement, and you'll be hard pressed to find one who isn't impressed by a student who pays the electric bill every month.

"Work doesn't really matter unless it applies to the major you are choosing or it helps to show that a student is really well-rounded. I would advise students to get involved in specific activities that do not interfere with after-school commitments, and I would have them relate their experiences in their job to an area of growth and have them write about that in their personal statement."

—Kathy Boyd
Head counselor
Canyon High School

"If a student needs to be working for financial reasons, then this is a story they need to tell to the college," says counselor Jennifer DesMaisons. "Most colleges are keen on finding a person with character and a good work ethic, and this sometimes is achieved more through work experience than through multiple, 'lightweight' activities." Consultant Judy Zodda agrees. "I think that admissions officers take into account zip codes and the possible need for a student to work to pay their own expenses, or even help out with family expenses," she says. "I also think it demonstrates responsibility if you have a job."

If a student has few extracurriculars because of work responsibilities, a counselor can be a valuable ally by explaining this favorably in a letter of recommendation. "If a student has to work to help the family, he or she shouldn't be penalized in the admissions process," says counseling director Leslie Kent. "The essay and the counselor's recommendation can counter any negative effects."

Thus, most of the experts surveyed here feel that work experience is viewed favorably by admissions officers, and that students can emphasize their work experiences in the same way that they can emphasize extracurriculars. However, not everyone agrees with this. Some experts feel that colleges really don't care much about work experience—unless, perhaps, the work relates directly to your future goals.

"Work doesn't really matter unless it applies to the major you are choosing or it helps to show that a student is really well-rounded," says counselor Kathy Boyd. "I would advise students to get involved in specific activities that do not interfere with after-school commitments, and I would have them relate their experiences in their job to an area of growth and have them write about that in their personal statement." "Colleges claim they view work experience [positively], but it has to be pretty major...for it to be equal to extracurricular activities," says counselor Lana Klene.

And while most experts are quite sympathetic to kids who need to work, others feel that high school is a time for more entertaining things. "My response to work is always that they have the rest of their lives to work," says counselor Kathy Stewart. "Get involved in extracurricular and or community activities and save the job for later."

ENDLESS SUMMER

What can I do during my summer vacation to prepare for college?

Charles, junior, Ohio, has been working summers for his dad's law firm, and he is hoping to be in the accelerated master's program for business

Summer's here and the living's easy. Three whole months to do whatever you want. But what exactly do you want to do? Maybe all or part of your summer is already planned out with a job, a family trip, or volunteer work in your community. All of those are good things, and all could, if you think about it, help your college admissions process along the way. You could also use the summer to explore schools during a family trip, learn a new trade through an internship, or research local and national scholarship programs. You could also go to a music or science camp, or maybe enroll in a college course and see how you like it. Ideally, you could do all or any of these things and more—but more than anything, try to find something that will not only pay the bills or offer some entertainment or education, but also get you on the path to college. It doesn't matter whether you're between your freshman, sophomore, or junior year. In fact, even in the summer after your senior year you can find opportunities to enhance and enrich your college experience.

"Do something productive that you also enjoy," says independent educational consultant Dr. Laurie H. Nash. "Visit as many schools as you can," adds counselor Ruth K. Littlefield. "If you go somewhere, check out if there is a college in the area." Even if it's not a place you've thought of going, you might be surprised at what you might learn and who you might meet, and in any case you'll get to see a campus in action. "Try to do something productive," says director of college advising Kate McVey. "If a student can have a week or so where they are doing something related to what they want to pursue in college, then that would be an ideal situation." "Be original, don't just enroll in a 'canned' program," suggests counselor Paula Porter.

Counselors emphasize that whatever you're doing, do something you enjoy. If you're in a job you don't especially like or if you're committed to a trip that's not exactly what you would choose, find ways to get more out of the situation.

"Do something useful," advises Paula Porter, adding that whatever you are doing, find time to "read, read, read." Counselor Gregory Rico says, "Make the summer meaningful. It can be community service, volunteering, job, internship, leadership programs, or enrichment classes on the college campus of interest." Many colleges have open enrollment policies in their summer programs. If it's not possible for you to take a course at one of the schools you're considering attending, try a class or two and a school closer to home. You'll learn a lot about both the academic and social sides of college life.

"Follow your passion; do what you love, and deepen a current interest," says independent counselor Ronna Morrison. There are many ways to do that. If you're a musician, for example, you could attend a music camp, or even teach at one. Otherwise, you could find work in a music store, set up or join a program to bring music to a nursing home, present a program at a meeting of a civic group, or work one-on-one with a musician to broaden your talent. Summer is a time for furthering your college—and life—plans. It's also a time for exploring and relaxing. Best of all, sometimes those can be the same thing: learning new things or fresh approaches to familiar ideas can be as refreshing as taking a complete break, sometimes even more so. "I tell students to continue doing something that they have been passionate about and not to just select some summer program that they or their parents think will be good for their record," says director of educational counseling Rachel Elkins Thompson.

FROM THE COUNSELORS

"I tell [students] to make the summer meaningful. It can be community service, volunteering, job, internship, leadership programs, or enrichment classes on the college campus of interest."

—Gregory Rico
Counselor
Highland Park High School

"Have fun. Participate in activities that will enrich you as a person. Read, read, read."

—Renee L. Goldberg
Director
Educational Options, LLC

"I tell students that they should naturally experience a change from their school year, whether that be resting from an intense schedule, or simply changing that schedule from academic to pragmatic," says director of college counseling Barbara Simmons. That apprenticeship with a local carpenter can teach you things about architecture you'll never learn in a classroom, and teaching songs to a group of eight year olds will teach you things you never knew about music, kids, and teaching. Most of all you'll learn about yourself. "Work, relax, travel, breathe," says educational consultant Nancy P. Maslund. "Working, taking a course, planning to read all of Jane Austen's novels—I emphasize to students that summer is a time for exploring on their own terms," says Barbara Simmons.

"Working, taking a course, planning to read all of Jane Austen's novels—I emphasize to students that summer is a time for exploring on their own terms."

—Barbara Simmons
Director of college counseling
Notre Dame High School

"I have only seniors so I tell them to spend time after graduation investigating wise practices, such as time management, credit card use, and developing good listening skills."

—Pat Hammett
Academic counselor

NETWORK!

Can networking help get me into college?

Claire, junior, Massachusetts, is popular and outgoing and is president of three clubs, and she wants to be a political science major in Washington, D.C.

You've probably heard of Facebook, Twitter, and other online networking sites. Judging from recent reports, there's a good chance you have a profile on one or more of them. If so, you should already have a clear idea of how networking works. Even if you don't partake, you probably know that the main gist behind these sites is that you say this person is your friend, then you find a friend of theirs who's also your friend, then a friend of that new friend's who's also into this band you like, and so on...before you know it, you have 11,325 friends based on shared interests, schools, etc. Well, when it comes to college and life in the working world, networking can really come in handy.

Will it really affect my admissions efforts?

It's possible. Many colleges have online forums or pages where you can talk with college admissions officers in a more informal way than a letter or phone

FROM THE COUNSELORS

"I think that colleges do use the knowledge they have of the high schools they visit to help them put that student or high school in perspective."

–Barbara Simmons
Director of college counseling
Notre Dame High School

"I think student networking is important to students when deciding whether or not to apply to a school. Familiarity helps."

–Nanette Umeda
Post-secondary counselor
Kaiser High School

call might allow. You can find present and former students at schools you're interested in—sometimes even professors too—and chat with them about the stuff that's really important to you in making a college decision, along with asking for tips on the most important things you should do when you apply. Networking is all about making and maintaining contacts. Your parents, teachers, and counselors know plenty of people, too, so feel free to ask them for help or recommendations. There's a good chance they might know someone who knows someone.

"I believe that contacts between college counselors and admissions officers are very important," says counselor Sarah Soule. "It's as important as making the match between the right college and the right kid." According to Carol Gill, keeping up these kinds of networks between college counselors and admissions officers is advantageous for both "the information" it provides and the students who can benefit from it. "We find that establishing relationships with college admissions officers can make a difference in admission or financial aid for a kid who really needs to be given a chance to show what they can do," says college advisor Helen Kunkel.

What about friends and family?

But it's not just your counselor's networking contacts that can help you. You might ask around among friends and find out about someone who attends the school you want to attend. Maybe they'll have a friend who majors in the area you think you'd like to study, and you can ask them, face to face or online, the questions that you most want answers to. You might join up with one of the online sites designed to help with college admissions networking, like Cappex or Zinch. And don't forget to ask your parents and family for their help and advice, too.

"I have my students evaluate their college experience and print their responses for current students to read. Contacting the students who are currently at the college they are considering has been very beneficial."

—Marilyn Petrequin
College counselor
Petrequin College Consulting, LLC

"If students and their parents have met the members of a college admissions office or faculty or administration and have been left a favorable impression, it can give a student a better chance to be reviewed favorably in the admissions process," points out director of educational counseling Rachel Elkins Thompson. "I think networking helps in situations where you want the student to get a second look," adds director of college counseling Kate McVey. "If a student is clearly not a good fit for the college, then no amount of networking will help. However, for the borderline cases it is nice to have the ability [to find ways to get that second look]," says McVey. This is where having made personal contact might help.

What about students at the colleges where I want to go?

It's not just you doing the networking, either. Take advantage of the nets others are throwing out to you. "I have my students evaluate their college experience and print their responses for current students to read," says college counselor Marilyn Petrequin. "Contacting the students who are currently at the college they are considering has been very beneficial." "I think student networking is important to students when deciding whether or not to apply to a school. Familiarity helps," adds counselor Nanette Umeda.

Networking is about staying in contact, sharing information and interests, and helping each other out. Those are things that everyone does everyday. Think about that in relation to what you need to know and where you are in your college admissions process, and you'll have lots of new ways to learn what you need to know to make your way through it. Years later, when you're that secure sophomore, junior, or senior in college, remember to give back and share what you've learned with that high school student looking to follow in your footsteps.

MONEY (THAT'S WHAT YOU WANT)

Where do I find scholarships and how do I get them?

Grace, senior, Georgia, feels like she has to work twice as hard as A students to get a B, but she is hoping to go to Georgia Tech

Along with deciding what to study, which colleges and universities to apply to, and how to present yourself to them, you'll also be thinking about how to pay for it all—and if you haven't yet, don't worry, you will soon. If you'll be able to live at home while attending college, you'll have tuition, transportation, and books to consider. If home isn't an option and you'll be out on your own, you'll also have to think about dorm or apartment expenses, food costs, laundry, internet charges—the list goes on and on.... Regardless of which circumstances you find yourself in, the fact of the matter is a pretty penny—or several billion pennies—will be needed to keep your college ambitions flowing. So, the million dollar question is: how will you, and your parents, if applicable, pay for all this?

The first thing to do is get together with your family or counselor and brainstorm about budgets for your college years. You should also brainstorm about ways to cover the costs. Counselor Nanette Umeda recommends doing research either online, through newspapers, or even though your parents' jobs, as sometimes companies offer scholarships to employees' children. There might be local civic groups, religious organizations, ethnic groups, and other organizations that offer scholarship programs; there may be national ones, too. Sometimes you'll have to write an essay or do a project or prepare a portfolio to compete for these, so it's good to start looking around early to learn requirements and deadlines so that you don't get left out in the cold.

Will scholarships cover everything?
One thing to keep in mind as well is that finding one scholarship to cover your entire college tenure is like the Yeti—an extremely rare beast. It's more likely that most of the aid opportunities you discover will be for small amounts, so

you'll need to do a lot of research and maybe end up putting together a package of smaller awards to meet all of your costs. Counselors recommend the internet as one big way of searching and gathering information about possible scholarships and other forms of financial aid. "Fastweb.com and finaid.org" are two places to look, says college advisor Helene Kunkel, "but [more likely], the bulk of financial aid will come from the college a student attends."

Where is the best place to find more information?

A thorough search through the college's website is always a good idea, as are conversations with financial aid staffers. "I always mention fastweb.com and finaid.com, as well as logging onto the specific college's website and checking out individual financial aid possibilities, and heading for large search engines like Princeton Review or College Board," says director of college counseling Barbara Simmons. "I generally recommend the College Board scholarship search, but will often help students search for interest specific scholarships as well," says director of educational counseling Rachel Elkins Thompson.

In addition to online sites, "the financial aid office of a college and your high school guidance office" are good sources of information, according to independent counselor Ronna Morrison. Barbara Simmons adds that she "also maintain[s] a Scholarship Resources Page that enables students to see the vast array of local awards that come in to our office." Many high school counselors do the same thing, so it's wise to ask and search online for these site, too. When asked what scholarship finding resources she recommends to her students, Ruth K. Littlefield puts it succinctly. "All!" she says. That's as good a place to start as any—good luck and happy hunting!

FROM THE COUNSELORS

"I always mention fastweb.com and finaid.com, as well as logging onto the specific college's website and checking out individual financial aid possibilities, and heading for large search engines like Princeton Review or College Board."

–Barbara Simmons
Director of college counseling
Notre Dame High School

Do I have to be a sports phenom?

If you have a specific talent, if you're from a certain area of the country, if you're going to major in a certain subject, or even if an ancestor fought in the Revolutionary War—all and more of these things may qualify you for aid from some program or organization, though it goes without saying you'll have to dig to find out about them. "I recommend that students be barracudas when it comes to scholarships," says counselor and teacher Mary Kovis Watson. "In Fairbanks, it is amazing how few students apply for our local scholarships. I ask students to consider it this way: spend a couple of hours putting this packet together, and it might bring you at least $500. That's pretty good pay!"

"I recommend that students be barracudas when it comes to scholarships. In Fairbanks, it is amazing how few students apply for our local scholarships. I ask students to consider it this way: spend a couple of hours putting this packet together, and it might bring you at least $500. That's pretty good pay!"

–Mary Kovis Watson
Counselor and teacher
Career Education Center—Fairbanks

Chapter 3
Everything You Ever Wanted to Know About the Application (But Didn't Know to Ask)

CHANGING THE GAME

How has the college application system changed?

Juan, freshman, California, feels like he's constantly in the shadow of his older brother who went to UCLA, and he wants to be a research scientist

It's a fast-paced world, meaning that change is inevitable—especially in the realm of higher education—so it's part of a counselor's job to keep on top of the daily, sometimes hourly changes in the college admissions process, while also keeping in mind the long view.

Is there more competition?

"The bar has been raised very high so that there is less predictability," for both counselors and students, says Joan Tager. "Because of the increasing number of students graduating from high school each year, there is more competition. Schools that used to be safeties are now as hard to get into as Ivies, and the effect trickles down to regional colleges," says principal Barbara Pasalis. Competition and more students in the application mix are themes that run through the experiences of many counselors. "Competitiveness has increased, especially at publics," says Bruce Barrett. He adds, "Financial aid has become more difficult to count on." Angela Conley sees that things have become "much more competitive and far more intense because of independent counselors and the demographic surge in applicants."

Despite applicants, families, and colleges all really being on the same side—that is, putting students at schools where they'll do best—these groups often end up working against each other, according to some counselors. "Families hear from the media and other families that the college process has become more difficult," says Ann Montgomery. "The panic feeds on itself, and students feel they must apply to more and more colleges." "Many students are applying to far too many schools," agrees Angela Badger. "The expectations are too much," says Autumn Luscinski. "Students are pressured to take an inordinate amount of AP classes." There's often more than one factor that's changed, too. Nancy W. Cadwallader points to a basketful: "Multiple applications, scores are unrealistic, competition...everyone seems to want the same school."

Are there more choices out there or is it just me?

"Families are feeling overwhelmed," concludes Suzan Reznick. And it's true—the process of applying and getting into college can seem like a labyrinth right out of Greek mythology at times. But another thing that's changed is that you have more choices when it comes to schooling—community colleges, regional schools, big universities, small colleges, and with the growth of the Internet, more ways to find out about them.

"Choose a school by its fit, not by its name," says Bruce Richardson. "Don't just look at a school because it is the most well-known." "Keep your options open," advises Angela Badger. "Start the process early and keep on track with deadlines." One reason to do that, according to Rebecca Threewitt, is that many colleges use online applications now, and the online process "can be deceptively complicated." She adds, "Many students are more intimidated than one would think by the online application process. With a few schools, a mistake on the online application can eliminate you as a candidate even if you are well-qualified."

Okay, are you scared yet? Don't worry, if you're prepared, you'll get through the process with the most flying of colors. "Apply early, prepare for the SAT and/or ACT, and remember—all four years count towards your GPA," says Carla Cruz. So despite things changing at such a quick rate, remember that with this change come increased options and opportunities—explore them all!

FROM THE COUNSELORS

"It is very difficult to predict, even from year to year, how a student may fare in the admissions process at particular institutions."

—Christine Asmussen
Director of college counseling
St. Andrew's-Sewanee School

"Try to have some perspective—there are dozens of schools where a student could be very happy and successful."

—Suzan Reznick
Director
The College Connection

FIVE—TEN—FIFTEEN—TWENTY?

How many colleges should I apply to?

Madelyn, junior, Mississippi, is in the top 5%, and she has heard horror stories about valedictorians not getting into certain colleges, and she is considering going into magazine journalism

You're doing a lot of brainstorming—noting what's important to you in a college, what you'd like to study, what sort of campus scene you like best, whether you'll need financial aid and, if so, how to get it. You're also navigating around all sorts of deadlines, forms, documents, essays, and advice. With all the things you're finding out, you might be wondering: Just how many schools should I apply to?

"I recommend at least six applications, covering a range of schools (top schools to less competitive)," says counselor Mary Kovis Watson. Educational consultant Nancy Gore Marcus finds that the number of applications submitted really "depends on the student." She recommends keeping the number of applications "between six and twelve." Barbara Simmons, a director of college counseling, says, "As a guideline—maybe three 'safety,' three 'probable,' and three 'reach' schools. A dozen seems to be near the maximum number that is

"Whatever number [of applications] is best according to what the student is shooting for."

—Ruth K. Littlefield
Academic counselor
York High School

"I usually tell students to apply to at least two to three colleges in each of the traditional 'categories' of admissions outcomes: likely to attain admission to, probable in attaining admission to, and difficult in attaining admission to. The biggest Do's of online applications is to have one's counselor or parent re-

view the application with another set of eyes to see if one has 'missed' something. The biggest DON'T is don't forget to print out any confirmation number or page after submitting online, and DON'T forget to keep track of one's online username and password."

—Barbara Simmons
Director of college counseling
Notre Dame High School

manageable." Independent counselor Marilyn Petrequin goes for a smaller number. "Six applications should do it, provided two are in the likely-to-be-admitted category and the student is satisfied with those choices," she explains. "We generally advise six to ten applications, in addition to any public in-state universities," says counselor Helene Kunkel.

It's another one of those balancing acts: you want to get into college. You also want to get into your number one school—the one that's strong in your preferred major areas of study, while having a highly acceptable price tag. Colleges want you to want them, too. Admissions and financial aid officers are looking to make sure you are a good fit for what they offer and what their community is like—much like how you're looking for the same things from your side of the table. So, when you're choosing where to apply, make sure you're picking places you would really attend. How many schools make your final cut "depends on how much students like their 'anchor' schools," says independent counselor Ronna Morrison. Counselor Pat Hammett recommends applying to "at least three—based on the entrance requirements, [they should be choosing] a dream school, a second choice, and then where they will attend if all else fails." Counselor Ruth K. Littlefield advises thinking first about what you really want. "[It's all about] whichever number is best according to what the student is shooting for," she says. "Sometimes one is enough if the student fits the profile."

What about online applications?
"Always use spell-check, but double proofread it as well, because spell-check does not always pick up obvious spelling errors," says Sarah Soule, a director of college counseling. "And don't write an essay that is too long as it will likely get cut off." "Don't submit after the deadline or wait until the 11th hour," says Helene Kunkel. "Servers always jam up, and you will experience anxiety. Do proofread, proofread, proofread before you hit the send button." Independent counselor Rachel Elkins Thompson is not a big fan of online applications. "I generally discourage students from submitting online applications unless they have no other option," she says. But if you're going to go the electronic route, looking at what you've written as a printed page can be helpful. "Print preview every application before submitting," says Ronna Morrison. "Remember to keep your passwords and user names in a file. Save while you are working online. Print what you have done," advises Barbara Simmons.

TIME OUT

How much time should I spend filling out college applications?

Violet, junior, Wyoming, is in the top 25% of her class, and she wants to study history

To become a competitive college applicant, you need to spend countless hours hitting the books, and then even more hours in school and community activities. But there's yet another time-consuming activity you'll need to complete if you want to go to college: the actual process of applying to college. Prepare to have one busy senior year!

There's quite a bit of disagreement among counselors on this question. Some counselors see the process as extremely time consuming. They compare the college application workload to an additional class students take their senior year, or compare this workload to a part-time job. However, others feel that students don't need to spend nearly as much time as they think thanks to on-line applications and other timesaving technologies.

Many counselors warn students not to underestimate the amount of time they need to spend on college applications. "The college process is long," argues educational consultant Rachel Winston. "Students who rush through and pop in answers without editing what they write tend to do poorly in the process because they do not take it as seriously as those who spend more time figuring out what they want to say."

In contrast, however, other counselors argue that the process does not need to be particularly time consuming—especially when it comes to filling out the actual application forms. Counselor Molly Tait estimates that students need to spend about four to five hours total on their college applications, while counselor Lisa Post estimates that students should spend about a half hour on each application.

Why so little time?

For one thing, online applications can make the process much, much simpler. In addition, as counselor Marie Soderstrom argues, the Common Application has shortened the process quite a bit for many students. The Common App is an application form that's accepted by more than 300 colleges and universities—with the number of schools that accept this form growing larger every year. Because more and more schools are accepting the same form, students don't have to rewrite similar information over and over again.

In addition, the Internet can cut a significant amount of time off the application process because schools have so much information online. Although nothing can replace an actual on-campus visit, students can use websites to find out more about schools and rule out ones that aren't right without visiting. One reason the process can seem so long is that students apply to too many schools, so ruling out choices can really help. Students can also find out quite a bit about schools before they visit by doing a little online research. That way, they'll already know what they need to see before they even set foot on campus.

How do I fit this work into my already busy schedule?

On this, counselors tend to agree: start early and spread out the work! By beginning the college search before senior year, students can avoid becoming overwhelmed by the process, and can use their senior year to focus primarily on writing a great essay and filling out applications.

"It seems to take forever, and it needs to be budgeted like a part-time job. For the really busy kids, [I've seen students] not applying to privates that might be good options because they're so tired," says Lynda McGee, college counselor.

FROM THE COUNSELORS

"The college process is long. Much longer than one would normally think. Students who rush through and pop in answers without editing what they write tend to do poorly in the process because they do not take it as seriously as those who spend more time figuring out what they want to say."

—Rachel Winston
President
College Counseling Center

How early should I start working on the process?

"Take advantage of school breaks in the junior year to visit schools," says counselor Keri Miller. "Talk to your school counselor during your sophomore and junior years to begin creating a list of prospective colleges. Also, students can get a head start over the summer before their senior year. Collect all of your necessary paperwork—social security number, transcript, honors, awards, résumé, letters of recommendation, and college essays—during the summer."

Guidance director Margaret King agrees, outlining how she recommends that students manage their time to keep the process from becoming overwhelming. "The search itself should take place mostly in the spring and summer of their junior year," she explains. "A finalized list should be done by September of their senior year. A folder should be used for each of the colleges with deadlines and requirements clearly listed on the outside. College essays should be selected so they can be easily adjusted to fit several colleges. Then it's just one foot in front of the other, making sure deadlines are met and that students are updating their school counselors on their progress."

Regardless of how much time students spend applying to college, admissions consultant Lloyd R. Paradiso encourages students to be excited by the process and not see it as a chore. "Here's a chance—for the first time, for many—to dictate their future," says Paradiso. "I would recast the question to, 'How much time should you spend on the thrilling process of mapping your immediate future?'" Say, that's kinda catchy.

"It depends on what your expectations are and how much you are invested in your future. This should be exciting stuff, not a chore. Here's a chance for many for the first time to dictate their future...I would recast the question to, 'How much time should you spend on the thrilling process of mapping your immediate future?'"

—Lloyd R. Paradiso
President and CEO
The Admissions Authority

PARENTS KNOW BEST

How active should my parents be in the college application process?

Maria, senior, Louisiana, works really hard to make her mom proud, but she thinks her mom might be a little too active in the application process, and she wants to be a nurse

Do college counselors want parents to be involved in the college application process? Most of the counselors interviewed for this survey strongly encourage parental involvement. However, a vocal minority feel that students need to do most of the application work themselves.

Many counselors encourage parents to offer their kids both moral and logistical support in tackling the long list of college application tasks. "I encourage parents to support their child in the process," explains counselor Keri Miller, "by offering to take college tours and being available to help answer questions or provide encouragement. They should ask questions, too." Counselor Marilyn Morrison agrees: "I encourage parents to offer support and encouragement, perform clerical functions, take notes and photos on college tours, and fill out financial aid forms." Educational consultant Marilyn G.S. Emerson encourages parents to help students brainstorm for their application essays.

FROM THE COUNSELORS

"I encourage parents to support their child in the process by offering to take college tours, being available to help answer questions or provide encouragement. They should ask questions, too. It is important for parents to be involved in the process early on. Meet with the school counselor during the junior year. Make a plan for the application process early. Decide who will be responsible for what parts of the process. Once a family plan is made, it's easier for everyone to participate."

—Keri Miller
School counselor
Minnetonka High School

"Parents are great at helping their child determine what qualities they want the college or university to know about," she explains.

Because the bureaucratic process of applying to schools can be such a nightmare, many counselors encourage parents to take the lead with the paperwork. "We encourage them to be the 'keeper of the deadline,'" says counselor Lisa Post. Counselor Leonora Saulino adds that because of budget cuts, her school no longer mails anything to colleges, so "parents are expected to mail transcripts and letters of recommendation."

A number of guidance counselors report that their schools have elaborate programs in place to help parents get involved. "We have a special program for the parents of 9th graders each year that lays the groundwork for the next four years," says counselor Margaret Lamb. "We want them to know what they need to do—beginning then—to have a competitive application package prepared by the 12th grade. We also make sure the parents all know what the pieces are that go into the actual application."

Other counselors take it upon themselves to devise a hands-on system to encourage parental involvement. "I have a mass e-mail list of every parent in the junior and senior class," says career counselor Sara Irwin Goudreau. She uses this list to e-mail parents deadlines and information about "what your student should be doing right now in the college process." Goudreau also holds Parent Night and Financial Aid Night for students and parents, along with making personal phone calls.

"I am probably different than most college counselors. I truly believe that it needs to be the student who does the bulk of the work when it comes to the admissions process. Ownership yields a quality product. I encourage parents to take students on visits in the summer and to discuss college finances honestly. Although I want to work with the student predominantly, the parents' support and the student's input are invaluable."

—Marie Soderstrom
Head counselor
Edmond Memorial High School

Or would counselors rather have parents let their kids figure it out for themselves?

Although most counselors prefer parental involvement, a few disagree and feel that parents should only be involved minimally in their children's college applications. Head counselor Marie Soderstrom says, "I truly believe that it needs to be the student who does the bulk of the work when it comes to the admissions process. Ownership yields a quality product." Similarly, admissions consultant Lloyd Paradiso warns that parents should maintain a low profile in the admissions process. "I urge parents to listen and not judge," says Paradiso. "I ask them to be involved as a source of encouragement, but not as a critic. Of course they have a say in the entire enterprise, but they should allow their child to spearhead and control the process, giving feedback only when it's solicited and stating parameters when they are important to the process. Otherwise, they should take a backseat and never refer to their own experience or that of a sibling. The focus is on the child in question."

Counselor Lynda McGee expresses frustration with overbearing parents who either do not understand the process or who do not have their children's best interests at heart. "I want them to understand 'fit' better," she says. "Some parents are overly involved in wanting to only steer students toward colleges they consider worthy, and others want the local community college only because they don't understand how financial aid works, or they don't want their daughters getting away from them."

On the other hand, educational consultant Rachel Winston defends parents who get involved actively in the application process—even if they appear to be a bit overzealous. "Most parents care about their children and want the best for them," says Winston. "While they are admonished by counselors and admissions staff regarding their 'ominous' presence, most just want to help. As long as they are asking questions and supporting the process, I want the parents to keep informed about their kids, have the latest information about what is important in the admissions process, and participate. Only in a few cases do parents become overwhelming, but even then, it is generally because they want the best for their kids." This is an important point—everything during this process should be done to ensure the best for the student applying. So if they feel that their college aspirations are taking a backseat to the hopes and worries of their parents—or anyone else for that matter—then it's high time to have a conversation about it.

EARLY BURLY

What to do I need to know about applying early action or early decision?

Alice, senior, Wisconsin, is in the honor society, has strong standardized test scores and is considering applying early decision at her first-choice school, hoping that will ensure her a place on the admission list

If you apply early action (EA) or early decision (ED), you can wrap up the admissions process while your friends are still sweating over essays and tracking down recommendations. Even if you don't immediately accept a school's offer of early admission—more on this below—"just knowing that 'you're going to college' relieves stress," says Leslie Kent, director of Leslie Kent Consulting. The majority of highly selective schools offer either EA or ED, and some even offer both. To participate in either one, you must submit your application by the early deadline. If all goes well, you'll know by New Year's whether you've been accepted (though there's a chance your early application will be deferred to the regular applicant pool, which means you'll have to wait until the spring, just like everyone else, to know whether you got in).

Are early action and early decision the same thing?

It's important to note that not all early admission options are created equal. Counselor Lana Klene writes that you should "make sure you understand the rules about these options" at the schools you're applying to, as different rules can apply to the same option at different schools. There are, however, some general characteristics of the two main options, early action and early decision. The latter is binding—you agree ahead of time to attend if the school accepts you. Because of this, you can only submit an ED application to one school (you should, however, submit applications for regular admission to other schools while you're waiting for the results of the ED app—you'll withdraw these apps if you're accepted ED). "I insist that the student visit the campus, interview, and do an overnight if possible (visiting classes as well) before he or she goes ahead with ED," says Barbara LeWinter, president and owner of Making the Grade to College. Counselor Eleanor Kinsella adds that a student applying ED "had better be in love with the school."

Early action is more flexible as you're not committed to attend if you're accepted. And, unless a school you apply to offers only single choice EA, you can apply to multiple schools via EA (though single choice EA schools still allow you to apply to other schools for regular admission). Students admitted to schools through EA can either accept an offer right away or wait to see what acceptances and aid packages they receive via regular admission, if they've submitted any applications to schools under that option.

Does applying early decision affect financial aid?

Another consideration when applying early decision is money. Jeanmarie Keller of Keller College Services describes ED as "not an option for a student whose family is looking for help to pay the bill." While students who apply ED can get financial aid (they're given an estimate of their aid package when they're admitted in December), they lack leverage to negotiate another package if the initial one offered is unsatisfactory since they won't have other aid packages to refer to and they've already committed to attending the school. Overall, the decision to apply ED should be "a family decision," says Lester Eggleston Jr., director of guidance and counseling at Lexington High School.

FROM THE COUNSELORS

"I make sure that students can stand behind why this is their first choice school. Has he or she really done their homework—visited the school, sat in on classes, visualized what it would be like to be at this place for four years?"

—Jennifer DesMaisons
Director of college counseling
The Putney School

Do I have a better chance of getting in if I apply early?

Finally, a note on admit rates. It's no secret that the percentage of students admitted via EA or ED is usually somewhat higher than the percentage of students admitted via regular admission at a given school. For any given school, you can "look at the available data to see what impact an EA or ED choice has on admissions," according to Leslie Kent. These numbers, however, can be somewhat misleading. Katie Small, a college counselor at The Princeton Review, says that "even though colleges typically admit a higher percentage of students from the early pool than they do from the regular pool, the students who apply early typically lie near the top of the school's acceptable range." While counselors generally agree that caution should be exercised when considering ED, they're divided when it comes to applying EA to boost chances of admission. Keith Berman, a certified educational planner, states that "not applying early means passing on an opportunity, and I rarely advise students to pass on an opportunity." On the other hand, Jon Tarrant, an educational consultant, says, "I never encourage them to apply early somewhere just to have done so."

"Early decision is for students who are certain of what school they desire to attend. I hardly have any students applying for early decision."

—Larry K. Kekaulike
Director of college guidance
Maryknoll School

UNDER PRESSURE

What is the most stressful part of the application process?

Leah, freshman, South Carolina, makes good grades and studies, but her parents are already pressuring her to research colleges and majors, even though she wants to go to school somewhere close

Without a doubt, high school students are more stressed than ever. Mass media may suggest that the biggest concern of most teenagers is to make sure they haven't exceeded their monthly allotment of text messages, but the truth is that college bound students are facing very serious pressures, not the least of which is the overwhelming terrain of the college admissions process. Just getting started can cause a major acne breakout.

Admissions consultant Leslie Kent says, "Students are intimidated by the perceived enormity of the process. They feel that it is much more difficult than it actually is. Some students deal with the stress with avoidance and they put off getting started until much too late. This, more than anything else, causes stress for the student and within the family. When I work with students, they say again and again, 'This is easy!' Getting started and having a sense for the sequence is the hardest part."

FROM THE COUNSELORS

"The biggest stress on students is their parents."

—Eleanor Kinsella
Guidance counselor
Dover-Sherborn High School

"This is the first time that most of these students will be judged by a group of strangers, and they know that the results will be very public. They not only fear that 'no one will want them,' but they fear that everyone will see their public humiliation. As colleges have begun to notify students of admissions decisions via e-mail, the fear of public humiliation has increased."

—Joan Bress
Director
College Resource Associates

Standardized tests?

After students have stopped procrastinating and actually started figuring out what the necessary steps are, the next thing that's likely to cause them to seize up with fear is standardized testing. Figuring out the order and requirements for taking the SAT, ACT, AP tests, and SAT subject tests can be as confusing as learning a new alphabet. Counselor Kathy Boyd says that her students find the most stressful part of the whole admissions process to be "testing timelines. They can't seem to remember everything at the 'right' times."

And once students finally do crack the code of which tests to take and when, there are the results to stress about! However, it is important to remember that testing is only one part of what colleges consider in the admissions process. College counselor Jim Prag mentions that his students perceive an "overemphasis of the value or importance of standardized testing." Director of college counseling John Reider agrees. He says that his students are unnecessarily worried about "standardized testing, because they think it counts more than it actually does."

The essay?

But once you've filled in the bubbles for all those tests, it's not quite time to put the pencils down. The factor that counselors most commonly cite as a source of stress for their students is the college admissions essay. Counselor Katie Small sums up the problem: "Although many students agonize about which schools to apply to, most of them fixate on crafting the "perfect" essay. Usually, that means hitting the thesaurus, detailing exactly how hard they work in each class, and 'discovering' how community service can actually help people. Because the essay is their opportunity to express themselves, they

"The essay is often the most stressful for my students because they often lack the clarity about themselves and their goals that would enable them to write a dynamite essay."

—Jeanmarie Keller
Director
Keller College Services, LLC

very naturally want to create essays that portray them in the most flattering light to colleges. Unfortunately, this results in students churning out essays full of the platitudes that they think college admissions officers want to hear, instead of a genuine expression of self." Of course, very few of even the most academically successful students have experience with this kind of writing. Educational consultant Whitney Laughlin says that the essay is hard for students "because it is not what they are used to writing in English class. Also because it forces them to be self-reflective, and not all teens are there yet—but the essay and college application process can be a wonderful tool to get them to do that!"

Waiting for acceptance?

Finally, after you've pushed past the procrastination, taken your tests, written your admissions essays, filled out the applications and financial aid forms and sent them off, you can enjoy the rest of your high school days stress-free, right? Of course not! Perhaps the most anxiety-producing part of getting into college is the wait between sending out the applications and receiving the results. Counselor Lana Klene says that the hardest part for her students is "waiting to see if they are admitted." Fear of rejection can make even the strongest applicants nervous. This is because of the "frightening numbers of students rejected or waitlisted at the most popular schools," according to educational consultant John W. Tarrant.

Is there anything that can help the stress?

Though there isn't much that students can do to get the colleges to send out their big and little envelopes any faster, there are some strategies to prevent the worst stress. If you get started early on understanding and actually beginning the process, take it one step at a time, and apply to several carefully selected, appropriate schools, you can rest assured that you've done everything in your power to make the process go as smoothly as possible. But if the stress of applying to college begins to have physical symptoms, you should take them seriously and consult your doctor.

STRESS TEST

How do I get through this process without going crazy?

Cooper, junior, Rhode Island, has worked hard for mostly A's while volunteering and spending time doing extracurriculars, but he isn't sure exactly where he wants to go, even though he hopes to one day go to law school

Okay, so you've got a lot going on. Classes, grades, extracurricular activities, your friends, maybe a job, not to mention your family and working toward your junior astronaut merit badge (well, maybe everything but the astronaut badge)! Combine all these factors with the many unknown quantities of applying to college—what they're looking for, what you need to collect to send to them, how to secure funding—and it soon becomes enough to drive a person nuts. Counselors have seen lots of students and parents through the college admissions process, so they know all too well that it can feel as though you're being pulled in a million different directions at once. Let's see what tips they have on how to get through the process relatively unscathed.

Does starting early really help?
Some take the practical approach. "START EARLY!" says Ronna Morrison. "It's the best way to keep your options open while reducing stress." Pat Hammett recommends that you "make a to-do list. Take things one step at a time. Don't be overwhelmed by the whole picture." Nancy Gore is also a fan of breaking what may seem like a never-ending process down into smaller tasks. "Complete one task at a time rather than becoming paralyzed by thinking about the whole process," she advises. Think about it this way: It's easier to break a boulder into pieces than trying to move it all at once. "Time management skills" are vital in reducing stress, says director of college counseling Barbara Simmons. "Laying out a grid/worksheet/calendar so that the deadlines do not creep up" is one way to help put those skills into practice, she adds. "Work on the process continually, leaving nothing to the last minute...[and] visit schools so that you learn what feels comfortable, and more importantly, what does not feel comfortable," says Laurie H. Nash. Post-secondary counselor Nanette Umeda points out that just talking with others can be a source of help, as well as a way to relieve some of the stress of becoming too wrapped up in your own situation. "I suggest students consult their college counselor for assistance,"

she says. "I also suggest they call [their prospective college's] admissions representative and see if they can meet when the representative visits the area. I also assure parents that they are not alone."

Keeping a grounded perspective is imperative. Part of this is accomplished by keeping the lines of communication open in the midst of all that planning and all those deadlines. "I encourage families to go through the process and breathe deeply," says Sarah Soule. "Take it step by step and think realistically while asking lots of questions!" For worried parents, Mary Kovis Watson offers these sage words: "Calm down. It is not so much where your student is admitted, but what he or she does once in college." She also points out that it's wise to apply to a range of schools in order to increase the odds of a successful college enrollment. Even though this may add to the work and the deadlines, it'll also increase your options, and that's another way to make the process work for you. "There are so many good colleges, try to have an idea of your top three instead of 'first choice,'" says Kate McVey. Helene Kunkel adds, "Don't procrastinate, that only makes the anxiety worse. Just plunge in and start doing the applications. Visit colleges early—don't wait until fall of senior year to start thinking about where you'll apply." She also recommends taking advantage of workshops your guidance office may offer on specific aspects of the admissions process.

FROM THE COUNSELORS

"Keep a sense of humor. Make sure you talk about other subjects than college admissions. Take good care of yourselves and relax."

—Renee L. Goldberg
Director
Educational Options, LLC

"Don't procrastinate, that only makes the anxiety worse. Just plunge in and start doing the applications. Visit colleges early—don't wait until fall of senior year to start thinking about where you'll apply."

—Helene Kunkel
College advisor
Palisades Charter High School

What do most students forget?

"I have always felt that the best stress reduction is knowledge," says Barbara Simmons. "So, the more a student and her parents know about the process through books, web resources, and working with the school's guidance counselor, the less stressed they will be by it all." Though the college admissions process can seem like a roller coaster ride or a bad round of dodge ball, keep in mind that there is fun to be had. "There's a college for every student—just relax and enjoy the process of finding the right one," says Marilyn Petrequin. Another important consideration, according to counselors: believe it or not, humor. "Keep a sense of humor," says Renee L. Goldberg. "Make sure you talk about other subjects than college admissions. Take good care of yourselves and relax." Remember: Just like the awkwardness of a first date, the stress of college application time will pass.

"Breathe and stay organized! There is a school for everyone."

—Ruth K. Littlefield
Academic counselor
York High School

COMMON KNOWLEDGE?

What do I do with Common Application supplemental materials?

Samantha, junior, Kentucky, is an artist and thinks she can get into art school with her portfolio, even though her test scores are lower than they should be, and she knows she'll need business classes in addition to arts because she wants to eventually own her own gallery

Put yourself in the shoes of college admissions staffers for a minute—they've got hundreds, more likely thousands, of applications to look at and evaluate in order to get a sense of the students behind the pages and decide who'll be the best fit for their school, both academically and personally. Maybe the college uses what's known as the Common Application form or maybe they have their own application. Either way, these forms are designed to garner as much info as possible from a large group of people, but what about the supplemental materials that schools allow? Should you submit any? If so, what should you submit? How much should you submit? Counselors have ideas about this that'll help you decide.

Antonios Lazaris advises you to start with the basics. "Ask the individual college as to what they may wish to see," he recommends. Bruce Richardson points out that supplemental materials can go a long way in showing a school

FROM THE COUNSELORS

"[What a student submits to the admissions office] varies with every student. It depends on a student's academic and extracurricular record. There is no set formula. It is crucial that each application be individualized to highlight the student's strengths; this is what will make it stand out."

—Barbara Pasalis
Principal
Northcoast Educational Consulting

who you are and where your talents lie. "Only provide information that will show the school a part of you that is not asked for in the application," he advises. Also, you can use supplemental materials to expand on something you've already written in the Common Application. "[Use this as an opportunity to write on] whatever hasn't been covered that will help explain specific circumstances to admissions officers," says Bruce Barrett.

What about a portfolio?

If you're aiming to study art, music, acting, or architecture—or anything related to those fields—you probably already know that you'll need to send along a portfolio of your creative work. But what if you're a top-notch violinist who wants to study biology, or aiming for a teaching degree while nursing a lifelong passion for the stage? Should you include examples of your other interests? "It depends upon the student," says director of college counseling Christine Asmussen. "I think that a student's talents may dictate [what they submit]. An art portfolio? An exceptionally well done piece of writing? Perhaps a CD if the student is unusually talented musically."

Supplemental materials are part of your chance to show colleges more about what makes you stand out and what you're really like, so getting someone to vouch for you is always a good idea. "Outside recommendations from mentors who know students in a context beyond academics are a good choice," says Angela Conley. "In addition, I encourage students to answer the optional 'anything else we need to know about you' question [on the Common Application] with a brief family context." Ann Montgomery suggests a way to highlight your strengths, whether those are in sports, science, or singing, by sending in "a one-page résumé, because it can be customized to highlight what is most important and representative about the student." Alison Cotten likes the

"Supplemental materials should include information that...has not been revealed in the Common Application. Just as students need to be well-informed before deciding which college to go to, college admissions counselors need to have as much information regarding the student in order for them to make the right choice as well."

—Barry Sysler
President
Academic Directions, Inc.

résumé idea, too, and adds another point to aid your chance of getting noticed: "I suggest students always mail schools a hard copy of their résumé, even if they already filled one out online."

When it comes to knowing how to apply and what to send, a view from the other side for the admissions desk can't hurt. Check out what the admissions staff within the Faculty of Arts and Sciences at Harvard College has to say:

"Each case is different. Harvard seeks to enroll well-rounded students as well as a well-rounded, first-year class. Thus, some students distinguish themselves for admission due to their unusual academic promise through experience or achievements in study or research. Other students present compelling cases because they are more 'well-rounded'—they have contributed in many different ways to their schools or communities. Still other successful applicants are 'well-lopsided,' with demonstrated excellence in one particular endeavor—academic, extracurricular, or otherwise. Some students bring perspectives formed by unusual personal circumstances or experiences. Like all colleges, we seek to admit the most interesting, able, and diverse class possible."

Wherever you fall in that range, it's the job of your supplemental materials to help make the case. What's the best way to do that? Send along "something creative and pertinent," says H. Allen Wrage, Jr. The best shot you have at showing a school who you are is by simply being yourself, and the best way to do that is by taking advantage of every opportunity you are given to do so on the application—advertise yourself! If you don't, who will?

FREE TO BE...YOU AND ME

How do I stand out to college admissions officers?

Faith, sophomore, Florida, is a talented writer and musician, but she knows her grades need to improve, and she wants to pursue a major that will let her be more creative at a school that will develop her individuality

"Be yourself," was the advice most frequently given by the admissions pros that we polled. And this applies even before the brochures start arriving in the mail. "When participating in activities," says counselor Tracie Morrison, "do so because you enjoy them, not to create a laundry list on the college application." Extracurriculars should be "limited to a few areas of interest that show strong involvement," states Carol London, director of counseling at Bishop McGuinness Catholic High School. And it doesn't hurt to "think outside of the box" as you pursue your interests, advises counselor Sheila Nussbaum. At the other end of the spectrum, working folk will be glad to know that a good, old-fashioned after-school job still carries weight with the admissions set.

Grades?

Of course, the best way to make you and your application stand out is to present a strong academic record. Sue Bigg, an independent educational consultant, believes that a lot of mileage in this area can be gained from "exchanging TV for studies." (Or the Internet for studies, if that's your diversion of choice.) Bigg writes that you should take the "strongest academic program available," which includes taking the "hardest courses your senior year," since admissions officers do look to see whether you're coasting as a senior.

Essay?

When it comes to the application itself, Tracy Spann, director of Spann College Planning Consultants, encourages you to "use the essay to reveal aspects of your life that are not fully described on your résumé or in your recommendations. Write it as though telling a story about yourself." As you compose your essays, "think of what makes you unique, what sets you apart, what is special about your values, your life, [and] your background," says William Morse, president of William Morse Associates. If you have trouble getting started, a potential source of inspiration could be **College Essays that Made a**

Difference, which is edited by The Princeton Review. The book features over one hundred real essays written by students who got into some of the most selective schools in the country.

Letters of recommendation?

In addition, Sandra Bramwell-Riley, executive director of Versan Educational Services, says that your letters of recommendation from teachers should be "exceptional." You should build relationships with your teachers, who, in addition to writing great recommendations, can act as mentors in your life. It's also a wise strategy to provide anyone who is writing a recommendation for you with detailed information on your accomplishments and goals as they pertain to the position for which you're applying (in this case: college student). Thank-you notes are always appreciated—in fact, it's best to think of them as mandatory since a little politeness today can really help you out further down the road.

FROM THE COUNSELORS

"Students should be able to articulate how they would contribute to the campus community, by virtue of how they spent their spare time during their high school years."

—Bill Kellerman
Educational consultant
College 101

"Look carefully at yourself. Be yourself."

—William Morse
President
William Morse Associates, Inc.

Attention to detail?

Throughout the application, Letitia W. Peterson, co-director of college counseling at Holton-Arms School, encourages students to "present their ideas in
their own voice, not in a way they imagine the college wants them to appear."
This doesn't mean, however, that the admissions process should be one-sided.
If you schedule an interview, counselor Stephen Newton recommends that
you should be "prepared with researched questions" about the school. And it
always helps to give your application a little extra TLC: All applications should
be "clean" and "neat," says counselor Cynda Wilson. And counselor Teresa
Knirck reminds you to "spell everything correctly" and to write "legibly" if
you're not using a computer or a typewriter (which you should, if either is an
option—in this age of technological wonder, the handwritten application has
become a bit passé).

"Students should spend quality time on fewer
applications, rather than spend less time on
more applications."

—Trey Chappell
Director
College X-ing, LLC

STRAIGHT FROM THE HORSE'S MOUTH

What do college admissions officers really want to see on an application?

Peter, sophomore, Kansas, is really strong in math and science, and he wants to get into a competitive engineering program

After spending hours slaving over that college application, you send it off and wait eagerly for a response. But what happens until then? After winding its way through the catacombs of the U.S. Postal Service, your envelope ends up on the desk of an officer in the college admissions office. The opinions of these folks can make a huge difference in your life, as these are the people who look at your application and decide "Snatch that student up!" or "Keep dreaming, kid!" So what do admissions officers want? Let's see what counselors report they've heard back about what college admissions officers want you to know.

Do I need all honors classes?

First of all, admissions counselors want you to know that it's important to take a rigorous load of classes in high school—even during your senior year. No, this doesn't mean you have to take every single Advanced Placement class, or that

FROM THE COUNSELORS

"Colleges have asked me to tell students to be candid and genuine. They want to gain a true sense of who they are and not what they think the colleges want to hear."

—Rachel Winston
President
College Counseling Center

you can never take a fun and easy elective (not that there's anything easy about ballroom dancing, trust us). However, admissions counselors are looking for evidence that you're willing to undertake challenging coursework on a consistent basis—evidence that you'll do well in college. As guidance director Michael Dolphin reports, "The transcript is the most important document influencing admission. Take the most challenging courses throughout the four years."

Straight A's?

Of course, just signing up for impressive classes won't cut the mustard—you'll have to do well in these courses, too. While it's true that it looks better to take difficult classes and not always get sky high grades than to take easy classes and always excel, a high overall GPA is crucial. "Grades are still the number one thing on which students are evaluated," says counselor Margaret Lamb. That said, "Be sure you have done something outside of class," she adds. "The more interesting, the better." Admissions officers appreciate a student who doesn't just set records in the classroom, but also in extracurricular and community activities.

A lot of extracurriculars?

Although involvement in a broad range of activities looks great on an application, involvement in one set of activities for which you have a passion looks fantastic. As dean of academic life Anne Weeks explains, admissions officers want students to "put their best foot forward by placing only the most important activities for which they have a passion on their application, not every little detail." Keep in mind that admissions counselors love students who turn in a cohesive package of materials, so if you've been the editor of the newspaper and worked on the yearbook—plus you took AP English and are excited about majoring in journalism—you've got a cohesive application.

"Make yourself stand out. Instead of writing a 'run of the mill' essay, discuss why you are different from the rest—what sets you apart, what will you bring to the college, what experiences you have that will make you a successful college student."

—Keri Miller
Guidance counselor
Minnetonka High School

A tailored application?

Admissions counselors also want you to know how to fill out an impressive application. First and foremost, they want students to follow directions. "If it says black ink, it had better be written in black ink," advises counselor Kerri Miller. Sounds nitpicky? Maybe, but think of it this way: Admissions counselors are very busy people and they're not going to look kindly at an application that takes them longer to read because it's filled out wrong.

Along the same lines, admissions counselors emphasize the importance of following deadlines and flawless proofreading. Schools don't want students who turn in papers late and full of typos—so show them that you're not that student.

Admissions counselors also strongly feel that it's important to research the school before you apply. Counselors don't want to read a generic application that's obviously the same for every school you're applying to. They also don't want to read applications from students who are obvious bad matches—and who would have known this had they done a little research.

Consultant Margaret King compares this to looking for a job. "If you interview for IBM, you read the annual report," she explains. Therefore, if you apply to a college, you should read their website and admissions materials. If at all possible, you should visit the campus.

It's also very important to turn in an application that stands out from the crowd and shows your unique personality. "Colleges have asked me to tell students to be candid and genuine," explains educational consultant Rachel Winston. "They want to gain a true sense of who they are and not what they think the colleges want to hear."

A stunning essay?

Counselor Keri Miller agrees, emphasizing the importance of writing a heartfelt essay that grabs the reader's attention. "Make yourself stand out," she says. "Instead of writing a 'run of the mill' essay, discuss why you are different from the rest: what sets you apart, what will you bring to the college, what experiences you have that will make you a successful college student."

One last thing that admissions officers want you to know is this: they take pride in their work and strive to make fair decisions. As consultant Lloyd R. Paradiso explains, "They are anxious to portray [their school] as a student- and family-centered place. They take great pains to explain the admissions process as fair, egalitarian, and ultimately in the candidate's best interest. Knowing many as fine human beings, I believe them, and urge my clients to do the same."

BEING AN AUTHENTIC CHARACTER

How do I show "authenticity" and "character" on my college application?

Sadie, junior, Illinois, has never been that good at writing and English and is really stressed about the essays needed for applications, and she wants to go to a large state school

We lost track of how many counselors urged students to "be honest" and "just be yourself" when responding to how students can show authenticity and character on their applications. The first part is easy, or at least it should be: Tell the truth.

The second bit of well-worn advice—"be yourself"—is equally sound, but it's not always easy. Not to get all philosophical, but what is the self, and when does it form? How do you be yourself when you know so much is expected of you, and you're afraid to let your true self come through at the wrong time on the chance you might blow it? These questions go 'round your head throughout the college-selection process, which is why it's so maddening. But it also gives you the chance to sum up all the components of who you think you are and who you want to be.

The counselors overwhelmingly agree that the essay portion of the application is the place where such amorphous ideas as "authenticity" and "character" can really come through. "The essay is the best place for students to be themselves and show who they are and what they really care about," says educational consultant Pearl Glassman.

And how do I be myself on an essay?

First, write about something you care about: it might be your father or how your city has changed since you were little. You can also select a political issue you feel strongly about, or an event that's been in the news recently. Do your research, as you would on any paper in which you have to construct a position and defend it, and then write it. Take weeks, if necessary, to think it over and make revisions. Read it aloud, and if a passage sounds awkward or strange, or sounds like something you would never say, redo it. Rewrite it until you're happy with it. Writing is writing, and novelists or editorial writers or college-app essayists all have the same obligation: to move the reader. And every professional writer will tell you that writing is rewriting—smoothing out the wrinkles until what's left is the picture that reflects what you want it to convey.

"The best way to exemplify authenticity and character would be through a real experience or through the discussion of an ethical issue," says counselor Rosa Moreno. "Being truthful about what was gained from the experience is very helpful." Counselor Yetunde Daniels Rubinstein adds that students should "spend some time during the summer writing personal statements that if their grandparents were to read, they would be able to easily identify who wrote it. Don't be afraid to brag about things you are proud of, such as helping siblings with homework every night, or the fact that they shovel their elderly neighbor's driveway all winter without being asked."

When writing about political or social topics, you must consider the audience (you wouldn't want to write about your devotion to all things hemp in an application for the late Jerry Falwell's Liberty University, for instance), but feel free to speak your mind. If an admissions officer is frightened by someone who's outspoken, that school isn't right for an outspoken applicant anyway. "Tell a specific story, especially how they might have changed their minds or opinion on something," says counselor Vincent McMahon.

FROM THE COUNSELORS

Should I get help writing my essay?

One respondent after another advised students to write their own essays, with minimal help. It's OK to have someone proofread for errors in style, grammar, punctuation, and overall consistency, but don't let someone else put their imprint on what should be your own work. A couple of counselors even had choice words for the many, many outside services who specialize in such endeavors. "Parents spend huge amounts of money and time to get an edge with a private counselor at the expense of spending time with their guidance counselors," says John Burke, who is, you guessed it, a high school guidance counselor. "Guidance counselors can be a huge asset to a student's application when they write their letters, which can illuminate a student's uniqueness and character." "Don't get caught up in books that show best-college essays or try to figure out what the college admissions staff wants to hear," adds counselor Joette Krupa. "They want to hear about you in your voice. Students need to trust themselves. Don't have every relative in your family and teacher you know make changes, because it isn't their essay, it's yours."

That's it, exactly. Your words are yours alone, and this is your chance to make a statement. Don't bother with a thesaurus. Even if you don't know a lot of sparkling synonyms, it's the quality of your message that counts. "Let the language and ideas be your own," says counselor Jane Mathias.

"I think it is all about the essay. I also find that some clients will not take the time to develop their thoughts and work through this process. It can take as long as a month to six weeks to work and rework an expression of your personality, desires, and authenticity."

—Janice M. Hobart
CEO
College Found

THINGS BETTER LEFT UNSAID

What should I not say on my college application essay?

Wyatt, junior, Georgia, has weak grades, but he is a team leader on the football and baseball teams—he isn't that sure he'll even go to college, though he would like to play college sports

What should you write about on your college application? The list of possibilities is endless—no hyperbole there—but here are a few suggestions: Write about your favorite book, flesh out a life-changing experience, or explore the most important challenge the world will face in the next 50 years. Maybe write about what students at this college can learn from you. If you could establish a national holiday, what would it be and why? Write about yourself and your goals, or maybe just your pet goldfish. These are just a few of the topics you might write about in the essay portion of your college application. If you're applying to several schools, you'll often find yourself writing different essays for each one, too, so fire up that keyboard!

The essay is a great way for admissions officers to learn more about you in terms of how you think, how you write, and who you are. You'll find lots of books and websites with tips on how to write and what to write about. Many of those sources advise you to be edgy and take risks to stand out. While that

FROM THE COUNSELORS

"High-emotion issues such as abortion, death penalty, etc., should be avoided. The readers may have their own opinions [on such issues]. Even if the student supports his views, the readers may react differently."

—Nancy W. Cadwallader
Educational consultant
Collegiate Advisory Placement Service

"This is a very individualized question. Any topic can be good or bad depending on the way it is handled in the essay. However, disclosure of indiscretions should not be the focus of the main essay."

—Barbara Pasalis
Principal
Northcoast Educational Consulting

can be tempting, keep in mind that there's a fine line between edgy and over-the-edge. Obviously, there are plenty of things you shouldn't write about.

Controversy?

More often that not, the essay prompt won't lend itself to anything too sala-cious. That said, be careful. "Stay away from topics that are very controversial, such as abortion," says guidance director Andrea Badger. "In general, don't give too much detailed personal information." One of the things that makes a good essay, college application or not, is wise use of detail. Using a detail here and there to give depth to an idea is great, but disclosing very personal information is not. "The essay is not a cathartic experience," points out edu-cational consultant Joan Tager. It can be easy to let emotions get the best of you and wind up saying too much about things that you probably shouldn't have. This is one reason why guidance department head Barbara Bayley says, "I worry about a student disclosing too much psychological info [in a personal essay]."

Guidance coordinator Bruce Barrett advises against including "Anything too far off the norm for adolescents. Colleges don't want to admit students who are going to create a disturbance on campus," he says. In their efforts to stand out, students sometimes lose sight of the fact that they have no idea as to the views and backgrounds of those who will be reading an essay. "While there are no absolute prohibitions, there are certainly many topics that would be a poor choice," says Suzan Reznick. "The obvious ones are those related to sex, money, and religious issues. The reader has to consider his audience very care-fully." "Being arrested or drug issues are probably not the best thing to write about," adds counselor Antonios Lazaris. Joan Tager also recommends that

"Essays should be marketing tools for the applicant."

—Barry Sysler
President
Academic Directions, Inc.

students steer clear of venting against the powers that be. "Blaming grades, school boards, teachers, or the system doesn't work," she says.

If you're beginning to think all this sounds a bit restrictive, think again. Professional writers never know for sure who is going to read their work or what their views may be, yet there are many thoughtful and engaging essays written all the same. Keep this in mind as you're writing yours—an essay, however short (and college essays should be short—imagine how many essays admissions officers have to read!), will succeed if it engages a reader with a good story and a strong voice. Think of writing your essay as having a conversation with your reader. Even better, think of your essay as a one-way interview—where you let the reader know why you would be such a valuable asset to their school.

Overcoming personal problems?

"Essays should be marketing tools for the applicant," says Barry Sysler. "Writing about shortcomings, failures, and moral victories do not serve the student applicant well." "Anything that would shock or cause outrage in the reader," is not a good choice, adds counselor Barbara Yeager. Counselor Alicia Curry says that "explicit details of sexual abuse or violence should not be elucidated." She also discourages her clients from "sharing mental illness or psycho-social challenges."

So now that you know what not to write about, how do you write the essay? Sit down, grab a pen or pencil and start brainstorming about what you could write about. Then hit that keyboard and revise, revise, revise—in the case of most writing, the magic is equally in the idea and the rewriting, so give yourself plenty of time and don't hesitate to ask your counselors, family, and friends for advice.

TO EDIT OR NOT TO EDIT

Who should I get to edit my college application essay?

Brody, junior, California, has always had an easy time with English classes and writing projects, so he's not really worried about the application essay, and he wants to go to a liberal arts school and perhaps study abroad

The college application essay is an opportunity for students to communicate a sense of themselves to admissions committees that goes beyond the test scores, GPA, transcripts, and résumé, to a more in-depth look at the student as a person. The essay is a place of relative freedom in the application—but many students are overwhelmed by the limitless possibilities, and experience a great deal of anxiety about what to say and how to say it. For this reason, most students rely on a number of people to read and edit their essays, both to get valuable feedback on basics such as grammar and punctuation, as well as to make certain that the point or message of the essay comes across clearly.

Counselor?

Often, college counselors see it as part of the important services they provide to help students with the application essay in some way. Independent counselor Tracy Spann explains her process: "I am one of the people who reads and edits my student's essays. I advise students to have their essays read and edited by three different people so they get a variety of suggestions and perspectives. I also advise them to make changes conservatively since it is more important for the essay to be written in his or her own voice." The types of suggestions that counselors are willing and able to make vary. However, since the college application process is within the special realm of knowledge in which counselors are experts, most agree that they can be of the most use to the student in the planning phase.

Getting started on the essay can be tough, and a common fear among students is choosing the wrong application topic. Counselors can be of service in this arena, since they have the experience of tracking many students' successes in applying to college over many years. Counselor Sheila Nussbaum says, "I will brainstorm ideas with students and talk about the approach they might take. I read for content—theme, voice, and how much can be learned about the student from the way they wrote the essay." Independent educational consultant Sue Bigg likes to help with the essay first at the planning stage, and then throughout the essay writing process. She says, "I do a lot of brainstorming. I tell the students when the essay is 'working' or 'wooden.' Towards the last draft or so, I may help change a phrase here or there and circle spelling and punctuation errors (I warn them about those homonyms the spell check won't recognize). I do request that I be the last person to read the essay. I am patient and creative and also don't have 30 essays plus 70 papers to go over each week [like English teachers do]."

Teacher?

Though English teachers are busy, they are a valuable resource for students writing application essays. Many counselors mention that this is an area where an English teacher might be best qualified to lend a hand. Counselor Scott Fisch says that at South Hills High School, where he advises students, "We have the Senior English teachers do this through a class assignment." English teachers are also particularly useful at the proofreading and editing stages of the process. Independent college counselor Jill Madenberg says that though she reads essays, "an English teacher is the best person to have edit." Similarly, counselor Steven Newton says, "I ask students to have their English teachers help them with editing for grammar." Other schools have special resources to which counselors are able to guide students. Counselor Bruce A. Smith says, "Our school has a Writers' Workshop where students can go for assistance."

In most cases, counselors agree that students should have several different people offer suggestions on their essays. Bill Kellerman, an educational

FROM THE COUNSELORS

"A teacher or advisor who knows the student well is the best person to review the essay."

—William Morse
President
William Morse Associates, Inc.

consultant, says, "The essay should be read by two or three people, including an English teacher and a person familiar with the topic." Counselor Tracie Morrison says, "I tell my students to have a few pairs of eyes read their essay, including parents, English teachers, and friends."

Parents?

Whether or not parents should read or edit application essays is a topic of debate among college counselors. Certified educational consultant Suzanne F. Scott says, "I feel parents should have some input." However, Sue Bigg requests "that parents don't even read the essay," as "they edit out all the personality." Counselor Sharon F. Drell agrees that parental involvement should be limited, but for a different reason. From her perspective, she says, "I do not recommend parents [edit the essays], as then it becomes the parent's work. Asking too many people can be a fiasco. Everyone has something different to say. The student should write a few drafts and then go back to it a few days later."

Myself?

In the end, the purpose of the essay, in the words of independent counselor Shirley Bloomquist, is to "provide a window into who [students] are." For this reason, "the best person to edit the essays is the student herself," says director of college counseling Letitia W. Peterson. She adds, "I often read essays and make suggestions, but the student should write the final draft." This is, after all, the student's essay, meaning that it's the student's opportunity to really show his or her own personality and sense of identity.

"The student is the best person to edit his or her essay. Most of the assistance I provide is challenging the student to think through their topic, to reveal what they're thinking and to avoid clichés and jargon. When they ask, 'What do colleges want in an essay?' I tell them the colleges want to get to know you! There is no best or worst topic."

—Valerie Broughton
President
College Connectors

RECOMMENDATION BLUES

What do I do about letters of recommendation?

Jack, senior, Florida, has always found it easy to make good grades and is a favorite among his teachers and coaches, so he doesn't think it will be that hard to get into the University of Florida

Getting accepted to the college of your dreams isn't just a question of a high GPA, enviable test scores, a high class rank, and a well-rounded showcase of extracurricular activities. It's the whole enchilada that matters, and letters of recommendation are a juicy part of this academic enchilada's filling. Make no mistake—letters of recommendation are very important. But when should you ask for them? Who should you ask? Do the admissions powers-that-be value one letter-crafter over the other? Ideally, you're good friends with that famed alumnus that just bought the college a new library. But that's not likely, so let's take a look at some of the above-posed questions.

When should I ask for letters of recommendation?

"At the very beginning of the senior year," says Dr. Dean P. Skarlis. "Students should keep asking teachers until they can find at least two [who will write them letters]. If they can't find anyone, maybe they should reconsider going

FROM THE COUNSELORS

"Students should find recommenders junior year, towards spring, when their teachers have gotten to know them well. I've never had a student who has been outright refused letters from every teacher, but if this were the case, I would push them to look for schools where a counselor recommendation is all that's required or where no recs are needed."

—Deborah Bernstein
Director of college counseling
Forest Ridge School of the Sacred Heart

"Ask teachers in whose classes you have excelled, shown great improvement, or have spent significant time working with the teacher to improve your grades."

—Ann Harris
Director of college guidance
Parrish Episcopal School

to college." Sounds a bit harsh, doesn't it? But there is a certain logic to the statement. If no one will go out on a limb and vouch for you, there may be a reason for it. If you find yourself in this situation, make sure you talk to your counselor and teachers to see if there's anything you can do to win back their support. It's most likely a problem with your grades or your behavior. If it's a behavior issue, straighten up and fly right—and make sure that the letter writers know it. It may not be too late to salvage your reputation. But if it's your grades that are flagging, get on the ball while you have time and raise them! There are several ways to do this. If you can afford it, hire a tutor. If you can't afford it, see if the class genius will cut you some slack, or join a study group.

Who should I ask for a letter of recommendation?

"Teacher letters are the ones that count the most," says consultant Donald Dunbar. "There is no substitute for letters written by those who have taught you in a classroom." This is because teachers are the ones who spend time not only recording your grades, but observing your behavior. And your behavior is a guidepost that points straight to your character. The best colleges accept candidates with high marks in academics and character.

What if I'm the sporting type?

Baseball, swimming, track, basketball, football, maybe even jai alai? You can ask your coach to write a letter. No, it won't be so much about academic grades, but the coach can tell admissions more about your capacity for teamwork and your leadership skills than anyone else on the staff.

"We tell our students to request one recommendation during the spring of junior year and then request others early in the fall of senior year. It's hard for me to imagine a student not being able to find someone to write a letter. I would say to start with the counselor and then ask math and English teachers from junior or senior year."

—Donnamarie Hehn
Director of college guidance
Canterbury School of Florida

"Those who know students well such as clergy, extracurricular activity monitors, and family friends make good recommendation letter writers."

—Angela Conley
College admission manager
SEO

"If they can't find anyone to write them a letter there is always their counselor," says assistant director of guidance Elise Ackerman. "We never say no. If a kid can't find two teachers to write letters for them, then chances are they are not going to be applying to schools which require them." There you have it—as a last resort, ask your counselor. Though they won't have had as much one-on-one time with you as your teachers, their letters are still respected by the admissions board.

What kind of information should be included?

At a minimum, a well-crafted letter of recommendation should include at least three elements. The first element, which opens the letter, should state how the writer is acquainted with the applicant and the nature of the relationship. For example, they could be your school counselor, a teacher, or a mentor in an extracurricular activity. Next comes an explanation of the applicant's skill set, accomplishments, and strengths. This should be phrased in a straightforward manner, without a hint of embellishment. Admissions officers read a lot of these and can smell dishonesty a mile off. The final part of the letter should summarize exactly why the letter's author would recommend the applicant. Once again, this section, too, should be straightforward, honest, and to the point.

How will I know this is all included in your letter?

Well, in some cases you might be allowed to read it, but in most cases the letter is sealed so you won't know what was actually written (this doesn't mean your recommender isn't singing your praises; it's just to ensure the professionalism of it all), so you'll have to trust your recommenders. This shouldn't be hard, though—they're pros. Most likely, they've been writing letters of recommendation for a long time.

NOW THAT YOU MENTION IT...

What do I want on my letter of recommendation?

Amber, sophomore, West Virginia, has tons of extracurriculars and really strong grades, but is not sure what her real strengths are, and she wants to go to a small school, maybe even an all-girls school

You know how the government occasionally leaks information to the media? It's a way for a person, or an agency, to get word out to the public about something they feel strongly about, without having to face accusations that they're tooting their own horn. Consider the letter of recommendation your way of "leaking" your best attributes to the college of your choice. If you've accomplished something you think makes you a strong candidate for admission, but aren't sure whether mentioning this will sound like bragging, let someone else do it for you! Teachers, guidance counselors, athletic coaches, and even bosses are usually more than happy to do it.

But there's a right way and a wrong way to go about getting them to write a dazzling letter of recommendation: After you've chosen someone who will a) remember how to spell your name; b) make sure to get the letter in the mail on time; and c) pump you up without overdoing it, you can make sure this person has all the information needed to do the job. Just as the White House will make sure a reporter gets all the data he needs to write a proper story, your recommenders will appreciate knowing all the pertinent details about you before they sit down at their computer or typewriter or stone tablet.

Do I need to supply information to my recommenders?

The vast majority of the experts we talked to suggest furnishing the letter-writer with your résumé, which should include sports, special accomplishments, citations or awards, and any other activities that could be pertinent. Others say a statement from the student about why this particular college is a top choice can be helpful, as well as background info about the school itself.

Joette Krupa, director of College Placement Consultants, says most of her students provide a résumé to letter-writers, because it allows the students to "show their interests in much more depth. For instance, the application begins with the 9th grade, but students do have a life long before then. If they have been dancing since they were six years old, a resume allows them to say it."

Some of the counselors we interviewed also suggest parents pass along "brag sheets," as well as newspaper clippings touting any noteworthy deeds. If you're an art student or an aspiring writer, letting the recommender view a portfolio of your work might assist them as well.

Though this may all feel a bit weird, this is one of those times in life when you've got to promote yourself. As the great pitcher Dizzy Dean once said, "It ain't braggin' if you can back it up." Mastering the etiquette of working with recommenders is a skill that will pay off for the rest of your life.

How do I ask?

Manners are important, however, because letter-writers probably are fielding multiple requests during college application time. Respect the recommender's workload. Most of the good ones already have a letter-of-rec template in place, so they can crank one out in no time since they know the drill. And word will get around about who writes the good letters and who doesn't, so the ones with a talent for it will often be deluged with requests. One thing you absolutely don't want is a teacher writing a letter that makes it apparent that they don't really know you. So make sure they have all the info they need. Counselor Cynthia M. Martini suggests giving a teacher a "résumé of your year in their class. Let them know about your experience in their class. By sharing this information with them, they can use it for your letter." Just don't call every five minutes saying you've forgotten to tell them about that perfect attendance award you received in grade school. Only pick those people who are likely to give you the most positive recommendations, too, because, as

FROM THE COUNSELORS

"Financial upheavals should be mentioned, if they will impact the ability to attend. Also, any unusual talents or abilities are nice to include."

—Glenn Ribotsky
Master trainer and tutor
The Princeton Review

counselor John Burke points out, "Colleges do not want to be besieged by too many letters. Students should be wary of 'padding' an application."

Can I use my coach?
Coaches also can make great references, because they know aspects of your character that aren't always discernible in the classroom: your toughness, your ability to work with teammates, how you focus when the difference between winning and losing is miniscule. It's a good idea to have a variety of recommenders to show that you're well-rounded, but still make sure they all know you and what your goals are.

"Any outside recommender (coach, employer, supervisor, etc.) should have personal experience with the student and write from that perspective," says counselor Jane Mathias. "All applicants should offer to have a conversation with a recommender so that the writer feels confident about what he or she has to say."

What if I've had some personal troubles?
Remember how we said the letter of recommendation can be used as a way to "leak" information? Well, don't forget that it can also be used to leak not-so-pleasant information, as a way of highlighting your successes against the backdrop of a hardship, such as a parent's layoff or an illness. "Extenuating circumstances or reasons for poor performance should be shared," says counselor Gloria Bond.

All in all, the goal here is to inform—the more you give you recommenders to work with, the clearer a school will see you.

"Artistically inclined students should take their portfolios or sketchbooks, writers could take small samples of their work, and athletes should take a list of accomplishments.... In general, providing a one-page résumé seems to remind teachers of accomplishments."

—Rosa Moreno
College counselor
Caracas Private School District

MAJOR DECISION

If I don't declare a major on my college application, will that impact my chances of admission?

Evan, senior, Tennessee, does well in all of his classes, and so he wants to take some time with different types of classes before declaring a major

When you're a high school senior, there's nothing wrong with being undecided about your college major. After all, you're 17 years old and you've never been to college, so how are you supposed to know for sure what you plan to study? But how will not knowing what you want your major to be impact your college application? Guidance counselors and other educational experts vary in opinion regarding this question. Some say that listing a major is a big advantage—or at the very least, it can't hurt. However, other experts argue that this doesn't matter at all, and that in some cases, choosing a major may actually hurt your application more than help it.

On one hand, some experts argue that it is important to state a major on your application because it's an important piece of information about who you are. As you write your application, you need to convey a clear and consistent narrative about yourself, and you can do this by choosing a major that complements your other interests. As educational planner Jodi Robinovitz explains,

FROM THE COUNSELORS

"It depends on the school. However, generally speaking, I believe that a student should at the very least have an idea of what they want to do or have it narrowed down to two or three areas. Focus brings clarity and clarity on the application can only be helpful to a student's chances of admission."

—Jeanmarie Keller
Educational consultant
Keller College Services, LLC

"I far prefer that a student has a 'hook,' a special focus that ties together the anticipated major with academic success in a particular subject and/or related extracurricular experiences."

Of course, for this reason, it's important that your major doesn't clash with the information on the rest of the application. For example, "if your personal statement is about your first experience with original science research, and you apply 'undecided,' there is inconsistency in the initial read, which makes it hard to understand you as a candidate," says counselor and certified educational planner Keith Berman. "The goal is always clarity."

Can I hint at what I'm considering?

Others argue that it's helpful to list a few prospective majors, even if you're undecided, in order to convey to the admissions office that you've thought about your educational goals. Experts suggest using statements such as, "Because I want to develop my writing skills in ways that are marketable in the business world, I plan to major in journalism, technical writing, or public relations."

On the other hand, many guidance counselors and educational experts argue that it's not important for a student to list a major on a college application. Many experts argue that students shouldn't be pressured to choose a major in high school, before they even know what majors might be available—and that most schools agree with this. As counselor Kathy Stewart argues, "I think that part of the college learning process should be learning about other options and learning more about yourself, which could mean a change in interests and a change in majors."

"I think students need to be honest. If they have to be anyone but who they are in order to get in, the school probably isn't a match. If a 17-year-old hasn't decided what to do with the rest of her life, that's okay."

—Leslie Kent
Director
Leslie Kent Consulting

Can it hurt my application?

Some experts argue that choosing a specific major on an application can actually hurt an applicant. Because admissions officers know that most students are undecided, declaring a specific major can come across as disingenuous. As educational consultant Leslie Kent states, it probably won't hurt to put down a major if you're genuinely committed to it, but if you put down something just because you think you have to, the admissions office will pick up on your lack of sincerity. "I think students need to be honest," argues Kent. "If they have to be anyone but who they are in order to get in, the school probably isn't a match."

Of course, if you're going to state a preference for a major, it's important to make sure that this major is actually offered at the school. According to educational consultant Whitney Laughlin, students write down majors the college doesn't offer more often than you might think.

Will a school tell me if it matters?

There is one thing that experts do agree upon: choosing a major on your application matters more at some schools than others. Therefore, it's important to research schools to get a feel for what they prefer. As college counseling director Jennifer DesMaisons points out, many smaller colleges emphasize learning across the disciplines, and therefore might be put off by a student who's already chosen a major. At the same time, some large universities may require students to choose a major (or at least a type of major, like engineering or liberal arts) because this will determine to which college within the university the student applies.

In short, there's no clear-cut answer as to whether it helps to put down a proposed major on a college application. Whether this is a good idea depends on the school. More importantly, it depends on what you really want. If you have a strong feeling about a particular major, you can use this to give the admissions office a better idea of who you are. But if you're thoroughly undecided—which many students are—being honest about this is probably much more advantageous than making something up.

FULL DISCLOSURE

Should I identify myself as an LGBTQ student on my application?

Luis, junior, Oklahoma, is considered a loner in school and feels like he is too different to fit in, so he wants to go to a school with liberal views and an accepting environment

Let's say you're a gay, lesbian, bisexual, transgender, queer, or questioning student and you're applying to college. Depending on where you stand, you may or may not be inclined to write about your sexuality on your application—and that's fine. There's no rule that dictates what you should or shouldn't reveal about yourself on the application; however, you might be wondering how it could affect your chances at admission. Counselors agree that regardless of your race, color, creed, or sexual orientation, it's important to find a campus where you'll be comfortable and thrive not only academically, but also socially. Needless to say, different colleges are known for different degrees of acceptance, so it's best to do some research beforehand to figure out where you want to go.

So, back to the question at hand: Should you mention your sexual orientation in the application materials, in the required essay, or when describing your involvement in extracurricular organizations? This is where counselors can be of different minds. Ann Harris feels that if the colleges really wanted information, they would ask for it. "Where do they ask [for a student to disclose their sexual orientation] on the application?" she asks, noting that identifying yourself with anything that not everyone accepts carries a risk. Andrea Badger says that what applicants should disclose "depends on the school they are applying to." She adds, "Some schools are more accepting than others. In general, I wouldn't recommend it because you don't know what the values of the person reading your application are." Barry Sysler has a different point of view. "Absolutely" disclose, he says. "It isn't about getting in—it's about the best fit." Autumn Luscinski agrees. "Students want to make sure that the campus to which they apply would accommodate them," she says.

How do I find out if a school is more accepting?

Counselors agree that this is an area where finding a campus community that's a good fit for you is important, but they have several ideas about ways to go about that. Also, it's a factor that should not be considered in isolation. Once you've decided what you'd like to study, you'll very likely be able to find campuses which offer those majors while also being LBGTQ friendly. "Disclosure on the application is less important than a visit to each campus to assess the college environment," says Barbara Pasalis. "It is essential to ensure that the college is welcoming to LBGT students." Angela Conley recommends doing your homework on a school as well, but also keeping in mind what purpose disclosure would serve. "It depends on the college and the context of the student's life," she says. "Several of my students who 'outed' themselves were admitted, but a few were denied admission. Context is the key issue." Carla Cruz veers to the side of keeping your personal and academic lives separate, saying, "Sexual orientation does not determine college success."

FROM THE COUNSELORS

"It is crucial to ensure that any school that they would be applying to would be a welcoming environment, but as to disclosing, I advise against it. I do not think that one's sexuality should be a factor in any admissions decision."

—Suzan Reznick
Director
The College Connection

"No, it is not a factor in the admissions process. They need to know if they will be comfortable on the campus, but that is not an admissions decision."

Nancy W. Cadwallader
Educational consultant
Collegiate Advisory Placement Service

All in all, just filling out the college application will require you to balance academics, community, your own personality, and lots of other things, all in the hopes that an admissions officer will find you to be the perfect candidate for their school. There's no right or wrong answer for disclosing your LGBTQ status, but think about how mentioning it will serve you. Thoughtful conversations with your counselor and other concerned adults in your life may be in order, and books and websites will give you ideas of ways to determine how gay-friendly a campus is, but remember that it's all about how you feel about things—your gut instinct—that should inform what you do.

"If a college welcomes diversity, then I think it can be appropriate to disclose, especially when colleges say they want authenticity from applicants."

—Alison Cotton
College consultant
The College Scout

"It all depends on the student's need to share and the individual school's reputation for having a liberal understanding."

—Antonios Lazaris
Secondary school counselor
East Hampton High School

LEARNING CURVE

Should I disclose a learning disability to colleges?

Benjamin, sophomore, Texas, has recently worked hard to overcome academic difficulties due to dyslexia, and he wants to be a doctor

If you have a learning disability, you probably know that the individual educational support you may have had in high school comes to an end when you graduate. You probably have plenty of questions when it comes to college, all of which start at: Should you tell the colleges you're considering about your learning challenges? Will this help or harm your chances at higher education?

According to counselors, maybe yes, maybe no. As with most college decisions, a lot depends on your goals, the schools you're looking at, and other factors in your situation. "It depends on the college and also how much help is needed once enrolled," says counselor Marilyn Petrequin. "It varies with the student and his or her particular disability," adds consultant Dr. Laurie H. Nash. This is a good point to have a discussion with your counselor and teachers since they'll be able to best evaluate your circumstances.

FROM THE COUNSELORS

"I think students should [disclose a learning disability] as schools that can assist students will take this into consideration. Colleges try to help their students be successful."

—Nanette Umeda
Post-secondary counselor
Kaiser High School

"I believe they should include it on their application because it can explain low grades and test scores, while also showing how resilient they are as to have overcome their disability."

—Gregory Rico
Counselor
Highland Park High School

What if it helps explain my grades?

You might want to let colleges know about your situation in order to explain spotty areas in your school record, and you may also want to find out directly from them what sort of support they could offer you and what the school's attitude toward students with learning disabilities is. "[Disclosure] often times will shed light on a student's academic performance by explaining a grade or academic trend on a transcript," says director of college counseling Sarah Soule. "Yes, students need to be honest, for their own benefit," adds counselor Mary Kovis Watson. "Perhaps the college has mediocre services. This all needs to be checked out. Colleges need to be up front with students and their parents as well." You should tell the colleges you're considering about your situation, advises counselor Helene Kunkel. She also recommends you "research accommodations available," as there's "no point going to a college where you can't be supported."

"I think that for a student whose grades are quite high and whose test scores are quite low it would be wise to mention a learning disability because it gives a reason for low test scores," says director of educational counseling Rachel Elkins Thompson. Kate McVey, a director of college advising, has another point of view. "Students should research the colleges they are applying to so that they can make sure the college has the right support for them. In terms of the application, the students should be admitted on their merits, not because of anything else." This is something to keep in mind: Are your grades and test scores good enough to be considered on their own merit? If so, how would bringing up your learning disability help or hinder such achievements? And if not, well, same question.

"In general, I encourage applicants not to disclose their learning disability unless this is needed to explain an uneven record or low test scores. If a student does disclose a learning disability, make sure that more than the learning disability is highlighted."

—Renee L. Goldberg
Director
Educational Options, LLC

Do applications ask about learning disabilities?

"I have not seen an application that asked for [students to disclose a learning disability]," says counselor Pat Hammett. "If asked they should respond; if not asked they shouldn't." Carol Gill, an independent counselor, adds that "Each individual case varies. I usually advise them not to disclose unless there is a compelling reason." However, educational consultant Nancy P. Masland offers a different opinion. "It opens doors [to students], and guidance counselors," she points out. But independent counselor Renee L. Goldberg says, "In general, I encourage applicants not to disclose their learning disability unless this is needed to explain an uneven record or low test scores. If a student does disclose a learning disability, make sure that more than the learning disability is highlighted."

How do I find out about support on campus?

What's clear is that you'll want to do some research on your own through college publications and websites, learning disability groups, and even by talking to other students during campus visits so that you'll know exactly what kind of support network—and how readily accessible they are—you can expect upon enrolling. You may choose to speak with a college's office of disability services, who will usually keep things confidential if you tell them to, or you may choose to disclose your situation and the questions you have directly to admissions staff. Or maybe you'll choose to do neither. In the end, it comes down to the nature of your own situation, how comfortable you are with it, and what you feel is the right way to handle it.

THE SOCIOECONOMIC TRUTH

What will my socioeconomic status do for me when applying?

Prudence, sophomore, Missouri, takes every honors course she can get into, but she will need a lot of financial aid wherever she goes

In the days of yore, a college education was the right of a privileged few who viewed higher education as a necessary springboard into careers in medicine, law, or the hip new field of aeronautical engineering. Thankfully, times have changed, so much so that "college" often rolls off the tongue as easily as the word "commodity." But while the attitude persists that higher education is now commonplace, available to people in all economic brackets of society, why do costs continue to swell so astronomically? If college is for everyone, why can't anyone afford it?

Quite frankly, in this case, money still goes a long way toward making a college education a reality. Counselor John Burke notes that "many of our wealthiest students work with private counselors who often 'manufacture' an insincere application for those students." Don't act so surprised. (Guess who also hires a professional to write their application essays for them?) Universities are businesses, too, and if they're attracting students who don't qualify for financial aid and who can pay it all in cash, they'll roll out the red carpet as far as it needs to go. That doesn't mean that if you're a student who will need financial aid you won't get in, but it certainly won't be as easy. The good news is that, in a way, thanks to students with no money worries, you might actually end up having more help from your counselor. Because those kids haven't a worry in the world, generally speaking, Burke says it "allows [counselors] time to work with those students with less resources."

Especially if I will need a lot of financial aid?

Although the temptation is to recommend the more affordable state-school route to those with fewer resources, counselor Yetunde Daniels Rubinstein stresses that all the possibilities in the search process should remain "open to everyone regardless of the financial situation." She says that it's more of a question of "how much of a fit the student and the institution are," than what their financial status is. The bottom line is, if you need the money, the money can be gotten. A strategy that counselor Cynthia Martini employs is to "tell all great students with wonderful grades that if money is a factor, they should apply to a school that is not as selective and that may offer them financial incentives to attend their school. They are in the market to attract those great students!"

FROM THE COUNSELORS

"The middle class student is in the most difficult position, as financial aid standards are at least twenty years out of date. Poor students can get aid—and universities think its PC to reach out to them (even if the students don't know it)."

—Glenn Ribotsky
Master trainer/tutor
The Princeton Review

Counselor Esther Walling's experience working with low-income students is that a fear of the expense of college causes them to want to stay close to home. "It's hard to get them to understand that financial aid is a real thing," she says, and that they can and should "explore new areas." Upon acceptance somewhere, sit down with your counselor and figure out how to wring the most money from the hands of the Dean of Admissions. Research all scholarships, from merit-based to need-based—leave no stone unturned, so to speak. If you're headed to a private school, inevitably you'll be filling out that FAFSA form, too—essentially the beginning of your debts to higher education. While daunting, the financial process can ultimately be as easy or as complicated as you make it. Don't be afraid to ask for help and keep in mind what you're working toward—a college degree.

"Financial aid is available to virtually every student on a need basis. If parents say they do not want to fund full tuition at private colleges, then we look at state schools or private colleges that will offer merit scholarships."

—Jennifer Tabbush
President
Headed for College

WHAT A LEGACY!

Does being a legacy student make me a shoo-in for admission?

Colton, senior, New Hampshire, is popular and active in extra-curriculars, and grades are decent, and he wants to go where his father and brother went to school, even though his test scores are too low

Most folks call it a "legacy," and it's one of those things that can be controversial, or not, depending on which side of the table you're sitting on. Maybe your second cousin once removed went to school at UCLA, or maybe your granddad endowed a building at Columbia University. All things considered—and we do mean all—the second scenario may get you a second look. That's because private colleges depend on private gifts for their operating budgets. Not that you or granddad can buy your way into a school anywhere. You have to make the grade, and meet the qualifications, on your own. However, if you're applying in the company of many well-qualified applicants, having legacy status might give you a better shot at admission. So what if granddad didn't have big bucks and he just went to the school? That may help you, too. Admitting a class of students is part of building a community, and whatever you can tell the admissions office about why you might be a good fit for their school will be considered. Considered being the key word here. This doesn't guarantee

FROM THE COUNSELORS

It depends on the college. If it is a University of California school, it means nothing. If it is Stanford or an Ivy, it means a lot."

—Marilyn Petrequin
College counselor
Petrequin College Consulting, LLC

anything—many legacy applicants are turned down every admissions season, as are many others—but still, any help, however slight, is welcome.

According to director of college counseling Sarah Soule, being a legacy applicant "could, in some cases, tip [the odds of acceptance] in the applicant's favor, but hopefully, the decision is first and foremost based on the student's academic record." "At some schools—and schools will actually tell you this on their website—legacy plays some part in admission, but it will not tip the scale in a student's favor if all else does not look positive in terms of the student fitting that college's applicant profile," points out Barbara Simmons. "Being a legacy can help at some schools, but the student still needs to be a qualified applicant," says Renee L. Goldberg. Gregory Rico adds, "I know some colleges give some consideration for legacy, however, it is really difficult to say how much they factor it in since each college is different."

Do I mention the family member on my application?

So, should you mention that distant second cousin of yours? How about granddad's donation? Why not? Unless you feel strongly against it, it's best to use everything you can to strengthen your application. But say what you say gracefully. It's an aside, not the main point. The main point, of course, is you. Your family is great and what they've done for the school in the past is laudable, but ultimately your chances of attending rely on your own skills, talents, and grades.

"Most schools are forthright about this. U Penn states that it takes more legacy applicants early than it will non-legacy applicants; other schools define legacy as parent/child and not sibling. It's truly dependent on the particular college as far as how much it affects decisions—but it does"

—Barbara Simmons
Director of college counseling
Notre Dame High School

Chapter 4
Interviewed, Accepted, Waitlisted, Denied

ADMISSIONS OFFICERS VS. ALUMNI

Which interview holds more weight in getting in?

Emily, senior, Delaware, works hard and makes good grades in English, but she struggles in history, and she wants to take advantage of the interview option for her application, because she thinks she presents herself better in person than on paper

This is a very nebulous question. Not all colleges require a formal interview. But for those that do require it, it's a sort of "feeling out" ceremony for both the school's admission board and/or alumni interviewer and the prospective student. The prospective student gains an insightful idea of everything that the institution has to offer—many details that simply don't come across in the printed literature—while at the same time, the interviewer can get a better feel for whether the student will be happy and comfortable at the college. In other words, will the student become a contributing member of the college community and go on to graduation and a successful career (a positive reflection on the school), or will the student be uncomfortable, jump ship, and seek scholastic satisfaction elsewhere? In the end, the results of the interview just might be the make or break factor for admission, but if given a choice (or not), who is it better to interview with: admissions officer or alumni?

FROM THE COUNSELORS

"I think there is too much inconsistency with alumni interviews. Recognizing that they are required for the top colleges, I warn students that some alumni ask unusual questions and that they should try to keep the conversation on why that particular college is a good match for them. If at a college for an interview, I remind them that they must have questions to ask at the end of the talk."

— Emilie Hinman
Educational consultant
Dunbar Educational Consultants

"Interviews with administrators carry more weight."

— Deborah Bernstein
Director of college counseling
Forest Ridge School of the Sacred Heart

Admissions officer?

It really depends on the institution's culture and policies. According to Dr. Dean P. Skarlis, president of The College Advisor of New York, "Interviews with admissions staff carry more weight. Three pieces of advice are necessary: 1) Research the school BEFORE the interview so that you can ask intelligent questions; 2) Be relaxed and be yourself, not who you think they want you to be; and 3) Send a brief thank you note or e-mail to the interviewer a day or two afterwards."

Alumnus?

While that opinion is certainly valid from an admissions office point of view, is there another way to look at it? Certainly! An alumnus sees things from a different angle. "I think the alumnus, as they listen from the former student standpoint, can tell if a school is a 'good fit' for the applicant," says counselor Debra Holmes-Brown.

So how does an alumnus go about the interview compared to an admissions officer? Once the alumni interviewer gets his list of prospective students, he or she schedules the interview appointments both at a place and time where both will feel at ease.

"Most colleges are not interviewing as part of the admissions process. I am not convinced that the more selective schools pay a great deal of attention to the alumni interview. It has been our experience that a recommendation from the alumni interviewer carries very little weight. Also, the alum really has no genuine idea what to ask a student to get a good view of them as a candidate. Many just use it as an opportunity to talk about their experiences at the college."

—Susan M. Patterson
CEO and director of services
College Placement Consulting

What sort of topics will we discuss?

The interview itself usually takes less than an hour. Interview topics are likely to include the following:

- What did you enjoy and what did you dislike about the high school experience?

- Which courses did you most enjoy (and do they dovetail nicely with your chosen major, if you have one)?

- What do you do during spare time? Sports? Wild partying?

- In which extracurricular activities did you participate in high school?

- Do you plan to continue this trend in college?

All in all, it's fairly painless, and likely to be less formal than an interview with the admissions office. Let's explore that side of the coin, too.

How will the interviews be different?

An interview by the admissions board is basically the same as the one conducted by an alumnus except that it's held in a more formal setting and the questions will come phrased in a more academic way rather than in a laid-back peer format.

The interview itself may be conducted by one person or a panel. This can be slightly intimidating to you, the applicant, but don't let it be. As counselor Dan Crabtree advises, "Be open, be honest, but don't try too hard to be cutesy, clever, or shocking. Be yourself, and let the interviewer see who you are, what you care about, and what you would contribute to the campus."

What is the best way to prepare for these interviews?

Well, think of an admissions interview just as you would a job interview. In fact, you might as well start thinking of college as a job right now. You'll be competing with your classmates for top grades now, just as you will for promotions during the course of your future career. Your GPA may be one of the defining factors when you land your first gig. It can relate to whether you get the job and what your starting compensation will be.

What are some tips for success?

- Dress appropriately. This doesn't mean suit and tie. Wander around the campus in the days prior to your interview. How does the staff dress? How do the students dress? You'll want to project the accepted student image, but spiffed up a bit. If the students all wear blue jeans and cargo pants, then wear a crisp pair of khakis to the interview.

- Anticipate the questions you'll be asked, plan your answers, and practice delivering them. Also, think of any counter-questions that might be appropriate. Nothing says you're on the ball and innovative as well as a properly placed, "Can you expand on that? How would it apply to this situation (give example)?"

- Remember to make eye contact with the interviewer. If it's a panel interview, cast your gaze around the crowd as appropriate, so they'll all know how attentive and interested you are. Above all, be yourself. These interviewers have likely been interviewing a long time and they can spot a fake one hundred yards off.

DRESS FOR SUCCESS

What do I need to know about the interview?

Henry, junior, Idaho, is the president of his class and plays two sports and still manages to make all A's, and he is excited about going to school on the West Coast because he's from such a small high school

So you've applied to a selective college, and now they want to interview you to see if you're a good fit. Eek! What do you do? (First off, don't go "Eek!") If you're nervous, that's understandable. Adults who have been in the working world for years can still feel insecure about interviews, and since this is likely one of your first, it's no wonder you might have a few butterflies.

Fortunately, interviewers understand that high school students don't have much experience with interviews, so they're willing to cut you some slack. What they're looking for is simple: They want to know if you're a good fit for their school. So the best thing to do is show them that you are. Here's some advice from counselors on how to present yourself on a college interview.

FROM THE COUNSELORS

"I tell students that they should feel relaxed. The interviewer is not there to trick them, but to help determine whether or not they will be a good match for the school. In order to best prepare for the interviewer, students should read through guidebooks, the website, and talk to students who have attended. If they learn more about the school, they are able to better know why they want to attend."

—Rachel Winston
President
College Counseling Center

"I tell students to be themselves, but their best selves. Shake their hands, dress better than they normally would, and look them in the eye. Remember to smile! Don't ever be late!"

—Lynda McGee
College counselor
Downtown Magnets High School

"Besides dress, manners are important. Eye contact and a good handshake can go a long way. Also, don't be afraid to talk about how fabulous you are—this is your time to shine.

What do I wear?

As counselor Margaret Lamb explains, "dressy casual" is probably the way to go. What does that mean? It means you don't have to go out and buy a power suit, but you should look professional. Think nice slacks or a skirt, a button up shirt, professional looking loafers or heels, possibly a blazer, and—that's right, gents—a tie. Everything should be ironed and neat, and avoid trendy looking clothing that's more appropriate for a high school classroom than a business setting. Think Macy's, not Urban Outfitters. Ask your parents to help you pick out an outfit, as they probably have a better sense of what "dressy casual" is than you do.

How do I hide my nervousness?

You want to assert confidence, which can be difficult going into an interview situation for the first time. However, by establishing strong eye contact, exhibiting good posture, and offering a firm handshake you'll look sure of yourself even if you don't quite feel it. Margaret Lamb reminds students to introduce themselves with both their first and last name, because this also conveys confidence. Just think of it this way: How would James Bond introduce himself?

However, one thing that's even more important than confidence is manners. Interviewers don't mind accepting someone to their school who's a little shy, but they certainly don't want to accept someone who's rude. Consultant Lloyd Paradiso encourages students to "be on time, be polite, look the interviewer in the eye, shake hands firmly, smile, pay attention, ask questions you care about, and listen to the answers." Counselor Keri Miller reminds students that it's always a good idea to send a thank-you note afterwards. And consultant Marilyn Morrison makes a point that is obvious but extremely important nonetheless—turn off your cell phone!

Always follow up with a thank-you note."

—Keri Miller
School counselor
Minnetonka High School

"First impressions do matter, so I advise students to not only be deliberate in making a first impression that is a true reflection of who they are, but one that they are confident in revealing to a complete stranger. Authenticity and integrity is most important."

—Yetunde Daniels Rubinstein
Guidance counselor
St. Peter's Prep. School

"Knowing about the college and knowing about themselves is most important for students. I had a wonderful client who constantly had his son answer the question, 'Who am I?' My initial session with him just knocked me off my feet, as he really could articulate his values, his passion for a career in medicine, and his love of sports."

—Janice M. Hobart
CEO
College Found

How do I answer the questions?

Counselors agree that what interviewers are looking for is for you to be your-self—your best self, of course, but yourself nonetheless. Counselor Lisa Post warns students not to make up answers—interviewers can see right through that! One thing that interviewers want to see is that students have a genuine interest in their school—and one of the best ways students can demonstrate this is by researching the school extensively before the interview. "In order to best prepare for the interviewer, students should read through guidebooks, the website, and talk to students who have attended," explains consultant Rachel Winston. "If they learn more about the school, they are able to better know why they want to attend."

After researching the school, counselors urge students to come up with a list of questions for the interviewer. As consultant Marilyn Morrison urges, "Do your homework and know something about the school so that you can ask intelligent questions." This demonstrates to the interviewer that you are serious about the school.

What kinds of questions should I ask?

Your questions should show that you know something about the school and are serious enough to want to know more. "Ask questions of the interviewer that are not obvious repetitions of the college brochure," says consultant Lindy Kahn. For example, a student might say, "I read about the engineering school's internship program online, and that sounds like a great opportunity. Could you please tell me more about the kinds of internships your engineering students take?" You can also ask questions about majors, college life, financial aid, the local community, and anything else that you genuinely want to know more about.

Moreover, though it's important not to come across as arrogant, there's nothing wrong with asking questions that help you decide if this school is right for you. "I encourage students to interview the interviewer," says counselor Marie Soderstrom. "I remind them that they are the client and that they have as much need to ask questions about the institution as the institution has to ask questions about them. "

Above all, try to relax! Yes, you need to take the interview seriously, but this does not have to be a situation that you lose sleep over for weeks. Remember, if the school wasn't interested, you wouldn't have an interview.

ACCEPTED! NOW WHAT?

How do I choose from multiple acceptances?

Jason, senior, Alabama, is the quarterback of the football team and has multiple offers for scholarships, and he wants to find a major that combines business and technology

Great news! You've been accepted—and accepted—and accepted. Wait a minute; more than one school wants you? If you think that's a good problem to have, you're right. But it involves some important decisions. Even if you're dead certain of which school is your top choice, it's time to take a step back and take another look at all the schools and their offers. Don't be surprised if you get a couple of invitations to school-sponsored events, either—colleges understand your need to make a decision so they'll be doing all they can to help you decide in their favor. Think of it as a job application, except that you're the one doing the hiring.

Another campus visit?

"Accepted applicants should always visit [the campus], attend class, and meet with professors and students," says Nancy W. Cadwaller. "Accepted Students' Day is one way of doing this and individual visits are another." This is especially true if you didn't have the chance to visit the school before applying, but even if you did, you'll be going back with a different perspective since you'll know that you might be living there for the next couple of years! This is one reason why counselor Joan Tager isn't a big fan of accepted student events, since they can sometimes offer a limited view of the school as a whole. She notes that it's worthwhile to schedule a "return visit" to the school, but do your best to avoid the "public relations" circus of "Accepted Students' Day." For a more balanced view of what things are really like at a school, she suggests "talking to friends who attend."

Suzan Reznick agrees, saying, "Accepted Students' Day is not the best day to make that final choice. It does not reflect the 'real' campus environment. Ideally, the student should try to go for an overnight visit to the dorms and attend classes." On the other hand, Barry Sysler points out a social advantage of going to a college's arranged events. "Attending Accepted Students' Day provides the student with an opportunity to meet other incoming freshmen in their cohort." "I strongly encourage students to attend accepted student programs," adds Angela Conley. "However, I also recommend they undertake independent research on the front end."

If you're not able to make a campus visit, see if you can talk with students or professors at the school, maybe someone involved in a campus activity that's important to you. E-mailing with students and professors is also a possibility, and though it's no substitute for being there, some colleges offer virtual tours on their websites. The key is to get answers to every question you might have. It's a cliché, but in a situation like this, knowledge really is power. The more informed you are, the more likely you'll enter into an enjoyable experience. Ann Montgomery offers this tip to narrow down your choices. "Add up the factors you consider important in choosing a college and assign weights according to their importance. Look at the totals. See how you feel when you see which school won out. If you find yourself disappointed that a certain school didn't have the highest total, then that's something to look into." One thing that all counselors can agree on is that there aren't any sure things in choosing a college. Ultimately, it comes down to a balance of practicality, information, and gut instinct.

Crunch numbers?

Since you're the one who will have to decide which institution's hallowed halls you'll be walking through, one of the things you'll need to balance is your budget. "Weigh your options regarding debt, attend Accepted Students' Day, and talk to current undergraduates," says Angela Conley. "Also, gauge

FROM THE COUNSELORS

"Spend a night on campus, attend classes in your major, review the cost of attendance, and attend Accepted Students' Day with [your] eyes open."

—Bruce Barrett
Guidance coordinator
Mascoma Valley Regional High School

"The more times a student visits a campus, the better able they will be able to make an informed and happy decision."

—Barbara Pasalis
Director
Northcoast Educational Consulting

your indebtedness against the college's record of employment placement." "Make a list of pros and cons," advises H. Allen Wrage, "then make a campus visit and talk to both those giving the tour and those not giving the tour." By taking in as many different perspectives as possible, you'll find yourself better equipped to consider what is truly important to you when it comes to attending college.

While this all may seem like a huge decision, keep in mind that it's really just a bunch of small decisions—each one you make will take you one step closer to knowing which school you want to go to. There's lots to figure out and lots to look into, but don't get too worried about it all. Christine Asmussen puts it in perspective, saying, "Do your homework, but remember that this is not the most crucial decision you will ever make. While you would hope to have considered all the important factors so that you will go to college for four years and graduate, if it doesn't work out, it is not a tragedy to transfer [to another school]." Going to college is an opportunity to learn who you are and become who you want to be—all while having a little fun along the way.

"If a student is leaning toward a school and has not yet made a final decision, then any visit they can make will help them in choosing the right college."

—Bruce Richardson
Director of guidance
Plano Sr. High School

TRANSFER STRATEGY

Should I accept enrollment at a college in hopes of transferring to another institution next year?

Mary, senior, Minnesota, has a bad habit of procrastinating, but she manages to pull off really good grades and high test scores, and she wants to go to a school somewhere warmer, but she's realizing that the applications are taking a lot longer than she thought, and she might not make some of the deadlines

So you didn't get into your first-choice school, but you got into one of your back-ups. What to do? Should you attend your backup school for a year or two, concentrate on acing your classes, and then try to transfer to your first-choice school? Or do you commit yourself fully to making the best of it at your backup school?

There's no clear-cut answer to this question, and educational experts have a variety of opinions. Some experts argue that if a student didn't do as well as they could have in high school, a year or two in college can give them the chance to prove themselves. After all, many students are late bloomers who don't excel academically until late in high school or college. If this is the case, transferring can give a student a second chance at a first rate education.

FROM THE COUNSELORS

"If a student is not accepted to their first-choice school, or if they were waitlisted, I sometimes talk with them about the idea of attending another school, working hard, having a solid record of college level work—and then re-applying. It's important that the student knows how that college treats transfers, at what rate they accept transfers, and whether it is a 'transfer-friendly' institution."

—Jennifer DesMaisons
Director of college counseling
The Putney School

"Some students go through losses, illnesses, or other highly traumatic experiences that affect their grades, extracurricular involvement, and overall performance in high school," explains college counselor Katie Small. "A transfer student with a solid freshman year has a greater chance of admission at a more selective school than a high school grad with below-average records." Guidance counselor Eleanor Kinsella agrees. "For many, the maturity card was slow in kicking in and they need to go to one school before another."

Is it ever a good idea?

College counselor Jennifer DesMaisons sometimes encourages students to attend a backup school with plans to transfer, especially if they were waitlisted at their first-choice school. However, she strongly encourages students who do this to research the feasibility of transferring to the first-choice school. "It's important that the student knows how that college treats transfers, at what rate they accept transfers, and whether it is a 'transfer-friendly' institution," explains DesMaisons. "All [of these factors are a] very important part of that decision."

Of course, with the rising costs of education, some students attend a school with the intent of transferring for financial reasons. For example, a student might enroll at a less expensive school close to home so they can save money, and then transfer to a more expensive school after. This strategy can save a student thousands of dollars and make an otherwise out-of-reach education accessible.

Why is it a bad idea?

On the other hand, many experts argue that attending a school with the intent to transfer is almost always a bad idea. As guidance counselor Karen Brodsky argues, transferring from one school to another can be very

"The student who enrolls in one college with the goal of transferring to another is likely to disconnect himself from opportunities at his original college, thus depriving himself of experiences that might have made his experience at the original college a positive one."

—Joan Bress
Director
College Resource Associates

disruptive. Adjusting to a new school environment is a challenging and exhausting experience for all students, and doing this twice in two years can take quite an emotional toll on a student. Moreover, as educational consultant Whitney Laughlin argues, it's often significantly more difficult to be accepted to a selective school as a transfer student than it is right out of high school.

In addition, many experts argue strongly against a student attending a school with no intentions of making this backup situation work for them. They argue that if students come to school with no intentions of getting involved and becoming part of the school community, they're asking for an unfulfilling experience. For one thing, there's absolutely no guarantee of acceptance into the first-choice school, so if the student hasn't made an effort to fit into the backup choice, they're stuck. Second, it's entirely possible that the backup choice is a better choice than the student first thought, but they'll never know it if their only focus is on transferring first chance they get. "It's a mistake to transfer with the intention of making the first school a launching pad," says counselor Jon Reider. "Go to the first school with the primary intention of making it work for you." Educational consultant Leslie Kent discusses an example of a student who didn't heed such advice. "One of my students did not get into her first choice and was determined to transfer," she explains. "She never gave her equally competitive and equally excellent school a chance. Her lack of involvement and her unwillingness to look at the positive experience she could be having have led to a very unhappy year. She chose her courses based on what would look good to her target institution and not on her interests. It is one of my greatest disappointments that I could not help her move past this."

What about transferring from a community college?
Although many counselors don't think that attending a school with the intention of transferring is a good idea, most agree that there's one exception: community colleges. One of the advantages of a community college is that it can allow less-than-stellar high school students the opportunity to raise their academic records high enough to get into good schools. In addition, the lower cost of community colleges allows students to earn credits that can be transferred to a competitive school at a much more reasonable price—meaning that you'll get a diploma from the school you want at a desirable discount.

So should you attend a college with the intent of transferring? Maybe, especially if the backup school turns out to be a poor fit. But be sure to give your backup school a fair chance, as you may not be able to transfer, and you may find that it's actually a better fit than you thought.

COOLING YOUR HEELS

How do I deal with being waitlisted?

Justin, senior, Connecticut, is the valedictorian and a star track athlete with lots of extracurriculars listed on his applications, and he has high hopes for making it into an Ivy League school, though he's already been waitlisted by his top-choice school

Are you languishing in your own special ring of waitlist hell? Maybe you are and don't even know it because the term is unfamiliar (the spellchecker certainly disagrees with it, but we promise, it's a real thing). So to begin with, a definition is in order here. Basically, the waitlist is the college applicant's special purgatory. It's the admissions office's way of making sure dorms and classes are filled up with happy students. Most colleges receive many more applications than they can accommodate, but they know that only a certain percentage of those they give the thumbs up to will actually accept and send in their deposits. So, waitlisting students is a way of hedging their bets to ensure they fill every empty seat. Basically, if you've been waitlisted, that means you may or may not be able to enroll depending on whether (or when) an accepted student declines to enroll at that particular school.

What are my odds of being waitlisted?

It varies from institution to institution. But for an example, let's say a school has 1,000 empty desks, but they know from years of experience that only three-quarters of those they send acceptance letters to will actually send in their deposits and show up. This means that of the 1,000 students they have accepted, 250 won't accept in return, so they need to have a pool of alternate students who can take their spots. This is the waitlisted pool.

Hard as it might be, if you fall into this pool, don't take it personally. "I tell students that it's the college's loss, not theirs," says counselor Dan Crabtree. "I even said this when I was director of admissions at a highly selective college: 'You weren't one who we chose to admit, and it's our loss!'" Indeed, it might not be the right fit, and it's better to find that out before you enroll at a school than after.

Can I avoid being waitlisted?

Well, there's no guarantee out there, but there are steps you can take. The earlier you establish a strategy, the better your odds are. Learn the profile of students that get accepted to your school of choice. Do they prefer students that were active in certain high school clubs and organizations? Join them and participate. Is it a very sports-oriented college? Go out for the team in your sport of choice. Do whatever you can to keep a high GPA. Does the college require applicants to submit an essay? Do your best on it and have it proofread by as many qualified people as possible.

Don't forget the benefits of a personal touch either. Visit the campus and make it known to them how serious you are about attending. Do your homework before you go by learning all you can about the institution so you can demonstrate that you're a worthwhile candidate. Talk to students and professors at that school. This will also ensure that you will know the right questions to ask.

But if, in spite of all your efforts you get waitlisted, try not to be too down and out—a maybe is always better than a no when it comes to college admissions. Besides, if you're working with someone like Susan M. Patterson of College Placement Consulting, you won't be "greatly surprised" because you will have "already talked about the possibility." Another good way to look at it is this way, according to Donna Fiori: "I try to help students to see that it may be to their advantage to be at a school that really wants them versus some place where they 'don't measure up!'"

FROM THE COUNSELORS

"It's not a competition, and hopefully my students understand that 'fit' is what we've been after all along. If they truly get that, then they're okay with the decisions."

—Dr. Dean P. Skarlis
President
The College Advisor of New York

"When a student has been denied or waitlisted at a school that he or she wanted to attend, I stress that many times the deferral was not about the student. I often tell a story that I was told by a Harvard University admission representative. She said that most students that apply to Harvard University deserve to get into Harvard University. They don't apply if they are not worthy candidates. However,

What are my odds of getting in if I do get waitlisted?

Not to put a damper on things, but the accepted estimate is that your chance, as a random student, of getting off the list and into class is only about twenty percent. Not great odds in anybody's book, so yes, a feeling of rejection is bound to set in. That said, the better prepared you are for it, the more able you'll be to move beyond it and focus on finding the school that's right for you. Director of college counseling Deborah Bernstein says that she "actually uses grief counseling skills in my approach with [rejected students]. I will usually ask them to shift their thinking to the positive aspects of their remaining options—what do you like about the school that accepted you, why did you have it on your list, what kind of student did your accepting schools value? This way, they can...reflect on their own values so that...they will have a clear idea of what works for them."

Ultimately—and forgive the cliché and/or potential pun—this is just another step in your learning experience. The best lesson you can learn from it? Keep swinging. As counselor Carrie Boettger says, "[If rejected], this is the first of many rejections in your life. You will learn from this and be stronger for it—don't give up!"

Harvard University tries to maintain a balance in its student body. One year Harvard may need tuba players or political activists, and another year they may need actors and hockey players. This means that the student that applies who is the tuba player in the year that Harvard University does not need tuba players probably won't get in. This does not mean that the student isn't worthy of Harvard University, it simply means that the student didn't fit with what the school needed that year. Thus, I stress to the student that the deferral is not a reflection on the student as a person. This doesn't always help. But sometimes the story does help the student look beyond the denial at other options."

—Deborah C. Curtis
Guidance counselor
Massabesic High School

WHEN LIFE GIVES YOU LEMONS...

How do I handle getting rejection letters?

Ruby, senior, Washington D.C., has really strong grades and test scores, but she doesn't interview well, and she has dreamed about a job in politics for years, but she's gotten a few rejection letters

The college admission process is far from predictable. To minimize the risk of not getting in anywhere, college counselors advise you to apply to at least one "safety" school—a school you're confident you'll be admitted to if you don't get a thick envelope from any of your first-choice schools.

Sometimes, however, even a school viewed as a sure bet won't offer admission. There's more than one reason this might happen. A student might not put all of his or her effort into an application to a safety school, and the school, receiving a sloppy application, may decide—assuming that it doesn't determine admission solely via GPA and test scores—to withhold admission. Jeannette Adkin, director of college counseling at the Christchurch School, says it's also possible for a student simply to "shoot too high" with all of his or her applications—including the safety.

FROM THE COUNSELORS

"We had a student get into three great schools—with aid—after she had been rejected by all schools on May 1st. It's not over till it's over!"

—Kathleen B. Grant
Dean of students
Catlin Gabel School

Do I have any options?

You should know that it's extremely rare to be denied by every college that you apply to if you are careful and thorough during the application process. That said, you do have options if your initial applications fail to yield an admit. Pearl Glassman, educational consultant, says that your first step should be to contact additional schools, "to see who still is looking for students" and "file a late application with them." If your college counselor cannot help you with this process, the website for the National Association for College Admission Counseling (NACAC) is a great resource. NACAC annually surveys admissions officers to provide state-by-state lists of institutions still offering admission, financial aid, and housing after the initial wave of applications.

If no school still accepting applications appeals to you, this would be a good time to "go back to the basics," says counselor Rosa Moreno. Were the schools that you applied to actually a good fit for you? Think about what you would add to a college community. Did your applications communicate this? As you consider these questions, keep your third- and fourth-quarter grades up. Vincent McMahon, counselor at Queen of Peace High School, also suggests "taking the SATs or ACTs again" if you feel that you can improve upon your current scores.

With a strong finish to the school year, you can reapply to schools for spring semester admission, or you can prepare to enroll in "community college to strengthen your academic profile" further, says Jane Mathias, director of guidance at Nardin Academy. Certified educational planner Jamie Dickenson describes success at community college for one or two years as "a wonderful stepping stone" to a four-year college or university. Additionally, certain community colleges serve as "'feeder' schools for specific schools," says

"I always tell every student: I started at a community college with a 3.78 unweighted GPA and graduated from USC. Nobody cares where you start, only where you finish."

—Esther Walling
College counselor
Jefferson High School

private college consultant Freida Gottsegen, and can also increase your chances of admission there.

A final option is to take some time away from school. Joette Krupa, director of College Placement Consultants, says you can "do something meaningful for the year while reapplying." Work, volunteer, and travel experiences are generally looked upon favorably by college admission officers.

SECOND CHANCES, SECOND CHOICES

What can I do if I don't get accepted into any college?

Karl, senior, Florida, finds it easier to focus on how things work instead of memorizing formulas, and he's worried that his grades will keep him out of a four-year college

What happens if none of the colleges you apply to accept you? It's not a nice thing to think about, but realistically, it's something you should consider. We're not saying it will happen, but you never know...it could. When it comes to actually being in this situation, there are two things you should think about: first, why you didn't get accepted; and second, how you feel about it. Those two views, taken together, will help you decide what steps to take next.

You, of course, are the only one who knows how you feel about this. Confused? Angry? Embarrassed? Indifferent? Maybe relieved, even? Any way you look at it, you do have another chance to take a good look at where you are, where you want to go, and how to get there. Having the opportunity for this kind of introspection is always a good thing.

Why didn't I get in?

You may or may not have any idea why you didn't get accepted. It really is true that there are far more students than there are places at the most popular and well-known schools, and it's also true that schools have different ideas of how to balance their incoming classes by interest, region, and just about any other criteria you can think of. On the other hand, maybe your grades weren't the best they could've been. Perhaps you missed an application deadline or dashed off your essay without much thought just to meet one of those deadlines. Whether your lack of acceptances is due to something you had control over, or something you didn't, there are ways to handle it. Educational consultant Joan Tager says that she would "need to know why the student was unsuccessful" in order to give the best advice, but in general, possibilities for the next step include "junior college, a post-graduate year, or community college."

Should I go to community college?

Guidance director Andrea Badger suggests several routes as well. "Consider community college and then transfer to a larger school after a year or two, apply to schools that may accept you conditionally, or write a letter to the admissions office explaining extenuating circumstances, if there are any." Though they don't explicitly discourage you from doing so, counselors point out that appealing admissions decisions rarely works. But if you feel your case is strong, get your facts in order and go for it.

Conversely, you may find that community college is a good place for you to start after all, says Suzan Reznick, director of The College Connection. "Many students mature late and colleges do understand this. There are many great community or junior colleges which offer these kids a chance to grow up before tackling the challenges of a four-year school," she points out. Even if you don't feel you need the extra maturity, the colleges might, and starting at a community college could help with academics, too. "Try a community college and establish a track record there," says Nancy W. Cadwallader, educational consultant for Collegiate Advisory Placement Service. "High school grades then are no longer as important." It doesn't always have to be a community college, either. "Sometimes unsuccessful students have to look at much lesser known colleges with more lax admissions policies so that they can transfer into a four-year college later," says Alison Cotten, college consultant for The College Scout. "The lesser known colleges are often wonderful places for weaker students to become academically successful." President of Academic Directions Barry Sysler adds, "There are many institutions of higher learning for C students. If they wake up late, they can commit themselves to be the best student they can be this time around, and then transfer to the college of their choice."

FROM THE COUNSELORS

"Transferring from community college, taking a gap year to reconnoiter, studying and taking the GED, or auditing courses [are all routes to consider]."

—Angela Conley
College admission manager
Sponsors for Educational Opportunity

"There is a college for everyone."

—Antonios Lazaris
Secondary school counselor
East Hampton High School

Any other options?

"Attending skills-building programs at private preparatory schools" has worked for some of her students, according to Sponsors for Educational Opportunity's college admission manager Angela Conley. She has advised students "who attend a vocational institution for learning discipline and from there transfer." To decide which of these paths seems best to you, consider your interests and goals. "If it's a matter of motivation, consider taking a gap year," says Ann Montgomery, educational consultant for Sage Education Group. "If it's a matter of learning differences, attend a program that can help. To prove that you can handle college level work, start with a small supportive program that has open enrollment." Simply put, find a place where you feel comfortable enough to pick up the pieces and work toward what you want.

"Go to a community college to establish a better record. Show a passion that wasn't able to be realized in high school."

—Bruce Barrett
Guidance coordinator
Mascoma Valley Regional High School

"Many students mature late and colleges do understand this. There are many great community or junior colleges which offer these kids a chance to grow up before tackling the challenges of a four-year school."

—Suzan Reznick
Director
The College Connection

Chapter 5

The Inside Word

DO THE RIGHT THING

What are common mistakes that students make?

Brianna, senior, North Carolina, spends a lot of her time doing homework, and she wants to be a meteorologist

It often seems that the college admissions process is a minefield of advice. College counselors, parents, teachers, friends, and even representatives of the colleges themselves all have admonishments to "be sure to..." and "don't ever..." Unfortunately, these tidbits, while intended to be helpful, can often contradict one another, giving students a picture of the process that looks more like a booby-trapped labyrinth than a map of a clear and straightforward path to success.

But the biggest pitfall is probably the most obvious. The loudest DON'T in the chorus of advice from college admissions professionals is "DON'T PROCRASTINATE!" Educational consultant John W. Tarrant notes that his students "often begin the process later than they should." No surprise there, as getting started can be difficult and there are plenty of places to get hung up along the way. In describing her students, counselor Lana Klene says "some procrastinate in

FROM THE COUNSELORS

"I wish my students would prioritize creating a relationship with their guidance counselor...creating this relationship is so important. Why? Guidance counselors have to write a report that essentially answers the question 'how college ready are you?' If you calmly collect some thoughts, write down some open-ended discussion questions, prepare a resume, and then set up a time to talk with your counselor, you are one-in-a-thousand, and instantly get the attention—and the rec-

ommendation—you deserve. Meaning that one student has a huge personal and strategic advantage.

—Keith Berman
Certified educational planner
Options for College and
Rudolph Steiner School

taking admissions tests." This can create undue stress if you have a bad day and don't get your best score on the first try, because then you may have to take a test again at the last minute.

Do I really have to start early?

Procrastination can also cause problems because students "do not start early enough and allow enough time to visit a campus so that they can get the most out of each college visit," says educational consultant Judy Zodda. She adds, "Some procrastinate until the beginning of the senior year or into the senior fall and think they don't need to visit until after they are accepted." Visiting campuses is an important part of assuring that a school is a good fit. Counselor Karen Brodsky agrees about the importance of visiting schools early. Though she says she "loves that students visit colleges," she also wishes "they would do more in their junior year and summer instead of waiting until senior year."

And of course, there is also the ultra-last-minute procrastination of the applications themselves, which can cause students to make careless errors that could jeopardize their admissions chances. Counselor Kerri Durney says, "I wish that students would read directions and not rush through applications." The bottom line here is that being prepared in advance for each step of the process can make the whole college admissions timeline much more manageable.

On the road toward college, there are many obstacles that must be overcome— things that students have to do in order to make the transition from high school to college. You have to take the required courses, get decent grades, score adequately on the tests, write the essays, and send off the applications. With all of these necessary steps, it is often easy for students to overlook or take for granted the most important task in the college admissions process:

"Many students, though not all, are too concerned with name brands, both in their wardrobes and in their college choices. Sadly this extends to some parents as well. I wish more families would approach the process with an open mind. They would discover that there are hundreds of wonderful schools out there that they have never heard of."

—Leslie Kent
Director
Leslie Kent Consulting

"Students define schools as 'good' or 'bad.' A good school is one that their parents have approved, their friends are also applying to, and is probably tougher academically than that student should have to handle. A 'bad' school is one that the parents don't like, the friends haven't heard of, and might be easier for that student to get into. It is sad and ironic that often students don't want the schools that want them."

—Katie Small
College counselor
The Princeton Review

selecting the colleges! Which school you end up attending is the biggest factor that will shape your college experience, but many students don't put that much time or effort into this consideration. College consultant June Wang Scortino says, "Many students do not consider college selection a very serious step for further or advanced higher education." Counselor Kathy Stewart wishes her students would "spend more seat time searching for the place that suits them best."

But aren't the colleges I've heard of the most the best colleges?

Because students don't often invest much time in exploring their options for different colleges, they can fall into the trap of assuming the best colleges are the most familiar ones. Counselor Jim Prag says that his students often run into trouble because they believe "that well-known colleges are the best colleges." He adds that they "do not spend enough time thinking about the kind of person they are so they could come up with a more appropriate 'fit' for themselves instead of just getting in to some 'brand name' institution." Consultant Joan Bress agrees. She says, "I wish that students could forget about 'name recognition' when they are searching for colleges. It is difficult for many students to accept that a college they have not heard of can offer them educational advantages that are equal to, or better than, known colleges."

Who can I trust for advice?

Part of the problem of negotiating the dos and don'ts of college admissions is knowing who to trust for the best advice. Certainly, deciding on a list of colleges and making the right choices to gain admission is a huge endeavor for the entire family. In the end, though, it is the student him or herself who will attend the school and who needs to make the transition into independent young adulthood. Head counselor Kathy Boyd says that too often her students are "leaving it in the hands of their parents to do most of the work. I wish they would take the lead more." Educational consultant Jeanmarie Keller expresses a desire to see students "being more independent. Too many of my students expect their parents to do the college process for them. You hear so much about the 'rebellious student,' however, as time goes on, I have more and more students incapable of making a decision on their own. It is not uncommon for me to have a handful of students each year who will allow their parents to make all the decisions."

Even the most caring and concerned parents are not often up-to-date on the latest information about applying to college, and counselors often cite parents as the source of unhelpful or even misleading information. Counselor Jack Shull says that a common problem that families face is that students are "applying to way too many colleges and not taking my advice. The students and parents feel that the more schools you apply to the better your chances are of getting accepted." According to educational consultant Whitney Laughlin, things might run more smoothly if students "take more control of the process and not be so passive." He adds, this would keep "their parents from trying to take over (it's like beating them off with sticks these days!!)." Though students should remember to consider all advice carefully, in the end, choosing to go to college and figuring out how to get there may be a student's first act as an adult. Remember, it's your education you're preparing for, so it's up to you to decide what to "do" and what to "don't"!

Here's an easy reference to get you on the right path:

DOS

Do it early, as soon as possible, or right now.

Do consider many schools you haven't heard of.

Do listen to professional advice.

Do it yourself!

DON'TS

Don't procrastinate.

Don't choose a school based on name recognition alone.

Don't neglect school visits.

Don't let your parents make all the decisions.

SURPRISE, SURPRISE!

What astonishing things have counselors seen?

Fernando, junior, Texas, has decent grades and visits his counselor regularly to learn more about the application process, because he wants to go to a large university, and he will be a first-generation student

When asked to describe their most astounding experience, college counselors describe a variety of experiences that run the gamut from extraordinarily positive to frighteningly negative. For many counselors, the most surprising and delightful moments are the ones spent aiding students. As guidance counselor Mary Pat Anderson explains, the best part of her job is "the excitement in a student when they get their first acceptance."

Other counselors report how moved they have been by their students' admissions essays. "I am always astounded by what students choose to write about in their college essays," says counselor Lynda McGee. "Some highly personal and traumatic experiences are revealed for the first time in many of them. I didn't realize how cathartic writing college essays can be for students." Similarly, counselor Margaret Lamb is amazed by the creativity students show in their essays. "We always encourage our students to think outside the box when deciding on their topic for the college essay," she explains. "One year, I

FROM THE COUNSELORS

"I was shocked when a student who had a perfect SAT score and valedictory status in her graduating class, not to mention also being editor of her school newspaper, did not receive admission to an Ivy League school.... Lesson re-learned: It is not possible to predict what college admissions personnel are looking for. Prepare the students for all possibilities. There is no such thing as a 'slam dunk' in the admissions process!"

—Marie Soderstrom
Head counselor
Edmond Memorial High School

had a student who wrote an amazing essay about attending an opera in China with her grandfather. It was so well written that I could envision myself there. The wonderful 'twist' at the end was that the experience was, in fact, only a dream! The student was accepted and graduated from Harvard."

Anything really shocking?

Since the most positive experiences relate to student success, it comes as no surprise that the most negative experiences come with student setbacks. When an admissions decision doesn't go as expected, it can be almost as shocking to a counselor as it is to the student. "I was shocked when a student who had a perfect SAT score and valedictory status in her graduating class, not to mention also being editor of her school newspaper, did not receive admission to an Ivy League school," recalls head counselor Marie Soderstrom. "I truly did not feel it would be difficult for her to get in. Lesson re-learned: It is not possible to predict what college admissions personnel are looking for. Prepare the students for all possibilities. There is no such thing as a 'slam dunk' in the admissions process!"

How do parents react?

Just as counselors report that their happiest surprises come from students, they also report that their most negative surprises can often come from parents. Counselors find themselves taken aback at times by parents' behavior. Admissions consultant Lloyd R. Paradiso takes issue when dealing with "parents intent on shoehorning their academic lightweight into a competitive college." According to Paradiso, it's far too common for a parent to ask him what schools he got his clients into. They fail to understand that students are admitted on the basis of their academic and extracurricular merits, and not on

"I am always astounded by what students choose to write about in their college essays. Some highly personal and traumatic experiences are revealed for the first time in many of them. I didn't realize how cathartic writing college essays can be for students."

—Lynda McGee
College counselor
Downtown Magnets High School

how costly a counselor's services are. Counselors offer expert guidance, but never a guarantee, to getting into college.

Are students and parents prepared for the application process?

Similarly, counselor Keri Miller says she's been shocked by how many parents actually fill out their children's applications and write their admissions essays. "If a student cannot fill out his own college applications or is not motivated to do so, that is a warning sign," says Miller. "[At this point], the family and the student should take a good look to see how prepared they are for college." Miller adds that this strategy is more than just dishonest—it's ineffective, as admissions officers can usually tell when an admissions essay was written by someone other than a student.

Fortunately, the counselors in this survey did not report the same complaints in regards to their students. However, many of them did report how surprised they were at how little their students (and their parents) knew about the application process.

One thing that surprised many of the counselors was how little students and parents knew about the work involved in applying to colleges. The arduous process of filling out forms, visiting and researching schools, and ultimately applying was something many students and their parents did not expect. "Many students don't understand the work required to find just the right school," says guidance director Leslie Munns. Counselor Martha Sharp agrees, explaining how surprised she is by "how little research and preparation many of our college-bound students and parents complete before their senior year of high school." Similarly, other counselors report how surprised they are by the number of students unwilling to fill out the necessary financial aid forms, and by the willingness of students to apply to schools they have not even visited.

By and far, the most surprising revelation we heard came from Anne Weeks, the dean of academic life at a private high school. Twenty years ago, she was quite surprised when one of her students was admitted into a particular school—because the student hadn't applied.

MORE SURPRISES

Are there a lot of great success stories or stories of huge disappointments?

Luke, freshman, Ohio, doesn't study that often, but he just saw his older sister go through the process, and he wants to have an easier time getting into a good school

Counselors and other education professionals who work year after year to help students to get into college have seen it all. One of the greatest assets they can offer students is the experience they've gained by working with so many students and colleges over the years. This experience allows counselors to draw not only on facts, data, and statistics, but also on real-life situations that help them to develop an intuitive feel for what is likely to be a good path for each student in his or her mission to find and get into the right school.

But despite their wealth of knowledge and experience, counselors are still surprised. Every year, there are particular situations that seem to contradict one another. Nearly every counselor has a story that illustrates the often arbitrary nature of admissions.

Educational consultant June Wang Scortino mentions the scenario of the "average student accepted by the U of Penn, while a good student is waitlisted at five schools." Jennifer DesMaisons, director of college counseling, tells about "being told by Yale that they admitted a student just because they 'loved' his application," and then feeling disappointed by "being told by Yale a year later that a different, even stronger student couldn't be admitted because he had no 'hook.'"

Then there are the stories that defy stereotypes and expectations. For example, counselor Jim Prag says that he is surprised by "how some athletes got into some of the most elite academic institutions," while counselor Kerri Durney has felt particularly rewarded for "helping a foster child get into a top tiered school." On the other hand, counselor Lana Klene remembers being disappointed when "one year...our valedictorian was waitlisted at Notre Dame."

What are their secrets for success?

Of course, most students hope to be among the one-in-a-million success stories that counselors sometimes tell. However, most of the time, counselors credit such successes to hard work and effort of the student, rather than to luck. Head counselor Kathy Boyd remembers these students the most. She says, "I have a student that got into Pomona last year and she was a student that had no parent help. She was so self-motivated and it paid off. I also had a student that got into the Air Force Academy and she had no help from her parents." Sometimes this hard work only leads to success after disillusionment occurs. For example, Barbara W. LeWinter, a private consultant, says that her "biggest success was helping a youngster recognize that there is not just one school that could meet his needs and help him realize his goals. After only applying to one school and not being accepted, I helped this young man plan a gap year and pursue his talents in photojournalism [and he later] gained admission to several schools."

This pattern of success coming from the dedication of the student is common among the experiences of college counselors. College advisor John Martinez tells about his greatest success story, a student named Spencer. "He deserves all the credit. This young man was frustrated by his mediocre grades and sensed something was wrong. Despite resistance from his parents, he contacted a psychologist on his own, described his symptoms, and then pushed for his parents to allow him to be evaluated. When his ADD was diagnosed in the spring of junior year, he took his medication and worked all summer to improve his organizational skills and learn strategies that would help him compensate for his weaknesses. His major essay was a compelling story of this journey and his grades during senior year were nearly all A's. We found a

FROM THE COUNSELORS

"Helping a student find a suitable match at an exciting 'reach' school is always rewarding. Unrealistic students and parents are disappointing."

—John W. Tarrant
Educational consultant
John W. Tarrant Associates

"Biggest success story was a student last year who got $155,000 dollars in scholarships, grants, and loans. He was relentless in getting good grades and seeking scholarships from the school and in the community. He will be only paying $5,000–$6,000 out of pocket for four years."

—Larry K. Kekaulike
Director of college guidance
Maryknoll School

college—several in fact—that looked past the numbers to this remarkable kid. He's very happy at the University of Delaware."

The flip side of this coin is that when a student has a lack of hard work, interest, or enthusiasm, they'll most likely find themselves greeted by disappointing results. Director of college counseling John Reider recalls "a top student who was admitted (and eventually matriculated) at Emory but was denied at George Washington because he hadn't shown any real interest in the school. He had not called, e-mailed, or visited." Barbara W. LeWinter had a similar experience with a student. She remembers the disappointment that resulted by "not insisting that a shy young woman learn how to be an advocate for herself and arrange an interview. This limited a number of her options since colleges viewed her reluctance as a lack of interest."

How do I deal with the uncertainty?

But no matter how hard a student works, and how much interest, dedication, and passion he or she has, and no matter how wise a counselor may be, there is always some uncertainty in the admissions process. Remember that top-ranked schools have to choose from an overwhelming number of qualified applicants, and are often forced to reject very good candidates. Estelle Meskin, a certified educational planner, recalls "when a super-qualified, athletic, artistic, leader who is living through Crohn's disease only got in to one of her eight schools, and [I knew] she would have succeeded at any one of them."

College admissions is an art as well as a science. Seeking the guidance of someone who has made his or her life's work out of helping students with the process can help to prepare you for some of the negative surprises, while increasing the chances that you'll be one of those memorable and happy success stories.

"My biggest disappointment is the number of students who are qualified but don't make it to the Ivies."

—Estelle Meskin
Certified educational planner

TIPS FROM THE TOP

How do counselors stay in the know?

Miles, junior, Michigan, has recently started doing a lot of research online, because he wants to go to a school with a good sports management program

Your counselors are the ones giving you all the advice and information about college—but how do they keep current on all this? And how do they keep up with all the deadlines, dates, and changes they keep telling you to stay on top of, too?

Books?

Educational consultant Joan Tager was one of those who gave us a look behind the scenes. "Every book I can get my hands on" helps her stay informed. She also looks to Internet mailing lists aimed at counselors' interests. Guidance department head Barbara Bayley also mentions "up-to-date books," and she keeps in touch with contacts in order to "share information with alumni and other counselors." Counselors Christine Asmussen and Suzan Reznick add that

FROM THE COUNSELORS

"I use The Princeton Review materials and books, **Peterson's Guide**, NACAC e-list, IECA e-list, along with any and every book I can get my hands on. College websites, conferences, college visits, comments of past and current advisees, and colleagues all come in handy. I also stay informed and current by reading The ISI Guide for my conservative Florida students, **Yale Insider's Guide, The**

New York Times, Wall Street Journal, Boston Globe, and Washington Post."

—Joan Tager
Educational consultant
CAPS

"meetings with college reps" go a long way in keeping current with the college admissions world.

Campus visits?

Counselors also do a lot of what they advise you to do—namely, visiting campuses, which is exactly what educational consultant Ann Montgomery does. While on campus, counselors will often be asking some of the same questions you would, plus some you wouldn't think to ask. This is a good thing for you since they're putting their years of training and experience to work out there on the college green, meaning that they might pick up on things that an observer with an untrained eye would overlook. Because of this, it's a great idea to ask your counselor about their impressions of certain colleges that they've been able to visit—they just might have a few nuggets of wisdom that could make all the difference in your college search. Those on campus visits also sometimes come as part of "attending professional conferences," which Ann Montgomery values.

Conferences?

Other valuable fonts of information for counselors are professional conferences, often held on college campuses or in convention centers, and organized by professional organizations to which many counselors belong. These groups offer lectures, newsletters, journals, continuing education info, and a valuable network of counselors across the country that your counselor can tap into when you need some background on a school in Seattle when you live in Charleston. Christine Asmussen says that "conferences and contacts" are extremely useful in staying in the know. Counselor Alicia Curry adds that college fairs, where many college representatives come to speak with counselors, are also a great venue for information.

"To stay current, I make college visits and telephone calls to admissions counselors, [and also consult] college websites for current events regarding grant moneys and where funds are being used, list serves with colleagues, and network at conferences."

Barry Sysler
President
Academic Directions, Inc.

"I talk with college recruiters, visit college fairs, and read all college materials that come to my office."

Alicia Curry
Counselor
Juan Seguin High School

Internet?

Of course, counselors spend most of their time in their offices—counseling you—so they value the Internet as a good place to research information they need. They often start with sites such as PrincetonReview.com, Peterson's, and the College Board. Most of these organizations also produce books that detail every aspect of the college search. One example would be The Princeton Review, which carries countless titles that relate to everything from **Cracking the SAT** to going to graduate school. One book deserving particular mentioning is **The Best 371 Colleges**, an annual publication that names the top colleges in the country and features more than 60 rankings lists and ratings. College admissions manager Angela Conley also recommends the **The Chronicle of Higher Education**, which has news reports and essays about college issues.

Admissions offices?

When it comes down to it, across the board, counselors find that "information from colleges directly," as educational consultant Nancy A Cadwallader points out, is the source likely to have the greatest reliability and the most information. Whether it comes to them in the form of handbooks, websites, e-mail updates, or visits from admissions representatives, "the universities themselves" are the best sources of information, says assistant principal Teresita Wardlow.

Think about all the tools that counselors use to keep themselves informed and apply them to your own college search. This is one situation, unlike, say, investment banking, where inside information is recommended.

THREE EASY PIECES

What is the most common advice that counselors tell students?

Seth, junior, Arizona, needs to work really hard over the next few semesters to pull up his GPA, because he has recently discovered that he wants to study geophysics

Plan, plan, plan—it should come as no surprise that that's the top advice from guidance counselors about the best way to get ready for college. Think that means poring over stacks of catalogs and browsing dozens of college websites? You may find yourself doing both of those at some point during your college prep process, but the first bit of advice from those who've helped hundreds of students sort out their college choices is more basic, and often, more challenging and fun.

"Think about what's important to you in order to be a successful student and a happy person," says director of college counseling Christine Asmussen. Counselor Rebecca Threewitt advises, "Take time to know your own particular strengths and weaknesses, and your preferences, before you become enamored with a particular school." Know yourself, and you'll make better choices and figure out your priorities more readily, the overwhelming majority of counselors surveyed replied.

In order to help you on this path to self-discovery, your guidance office will most likely have tests and questionnaires that you can take which will match your skills and personality with certain fields. However, keep in mind that these are just tools to help you and not rigid guidelines. Your best ideas about knowing yourself will come from looking at what interests you most. What do you spend your free time doing? What would you like to know more about? These interests will help you stand out to college admissions officers, too. "Think about what you enjoy when selecting community service and extracurricular activities," counselor Barbara Yeager advises. She has another point worth considering as you face the academic and personal demands of doing well in your classes, fitting in those extracurricular activities, and maybe even adding in a job. "Choose a healthy lifestyle," she says.

Okay, so you need to take some time to know yourself, your personality, and your interests. Counselors also point out that you need to know your stuff academically, and make sure the colleges know you know it, too. "Grades count even freshman year," advises guidance department head Barbara Bayley. "SATs do matter." Nancy W. Cadwallader, educational consultant for the Collegiate Advisory Placement Service, points out that it's not just about grades and scores, either. "Take the most rigorous curriculum that you can be successful in," she says. "Take AP courses if available." When it comes to extracurricular activities, "become a leader." It's important to show effort, interest, and do well. "Do the most you can with what you have, always seeking to expand your intellectual base," says counselor Angela Conley, college admission manager for Sponsors for Educational Opportunity. "Take challenging classes in the 12th grade," adds Alison Cotton, consultant for The College Scout. "Colleges are using the senior schedule more heavily in admissions decisions now."

Counselors also point out that to make sure all this work is noticeable to college admissions officers, you should start your preparations early. "Start applying early—start researching schools in your junior year," says assistant principal Teresita Wardlow. "Start the process early and keep your options open," affirms guidance director Andrea Badger. "Start working on your personal statement the summer before your senior year," says Barry Sysler, president of Academic Directions. Director of college guidance Ann Harris adds that you should "talk to your parents about your financial situation right now, so there will be no surprises."

FROM THE COUNSELORS

"Don't live for your transcript. Follow your interests and have a life!"

—Ann Montgomery
Educational consultant
Sage Educational Group, LLC

"Know that there is a college that will be a perfect match."

—Autumn Luscinski
Dean of students/college counselor
Pacifica Christian High School

Right, so you're getting all your ducks in a row: keeping your grades up, doing the extracurricular thing, knowing yourself and writing about that in your personal statement, giving college officials a great picture of you and where you are in your life. But you probably want a picture of what it'd be like to be on campus for the next few years of your life, too. The best way to do that is "visit, visit, visit" according to Andrea Badger. Joan Tager, educational consultant for CAPS, concurs. "Start visiting during your junior year," she suggests. "Visit campuses to compare," says Bruce Barrett, and then "visit your top choices two or three times to get the best picture and advocate for yourself," he adds. "Use your networks, and keep applying for scholarships," Angela Conley advises. You'll learn a lot on these visits, and you'll need to think it over. "Choose a school that fits you, and not just by its name," says guidance coordinator Bruce Richardson. The College Connection's director Suzan Reznick adds, "Try to have some perspective, because there are dozens of schools out there where you could be very happy." That said, "if you have a dream school or two, go ahead and apply," says Ann Montgomery, consultant for Sage Educational Group. "Never say never" about anything in the college admissions process, she adds. And of course, "meet with your guidance counselor regularly and keep up with deadlines," adds counselor Autumn Luscinski.

"Go to a school where you can get involved."
—Alicia Curry
Counselor
Juan Seguin High School

"Do the most you can with what you have, always seeking to expand your intellectual base."

—Angela Conley
College admission manager
Sponsors for Educational Opportunity

Notes

Notes

Navigate College with
Directions from the Experts

Find the Right School

Best 371 Colleges, 2010 Edition
978-0-375-42938-5 • $22.99/C$27.99

**Best Northeastern Colleges,
2010 Edition**
978-0-375-42939-2 • $16.99/C$21.99

**Complete Book of Colleges,
2010 Edition**
978-0-375-42940-8 • $26.99/C$33.99

**Guide to College Majors,
2010 Edition**
978-0-375-42969-9 • $21.00/C$25.95

College Navigator
978-0-375-76583-4 • $12.95/C$16.00

**America's Best Value Colleges,
2008 Edition**
978-0-375-76601-5 • $18.95/C$24.95

Guide to College Visits
978-0-375-76600-8 • $20.00/C$25.00

Get In

Cracking the SAT, 2010 Edition
978-0-375-42922-4 • $21.99/C$26.99

**Cracking the SAT with DVD,
2010 Edition**
978-0-375-42923-1 • $34.99/C$42.99

ACT or SAT
978-0-375-42924-8 • $15.99/C$19.99

1,296 ACT Practice Questions
978-0-375-42902-6 • $19.00/C$22.00

**11 Practice Tests for the SAT and
PSAT, 2010 Edition**
978-0-375-42934-7 • $22.99/C$27.99

Cracking the ACT, 2010 Edition
978-0-375-42962-0 • $19.99/C$24.99

**Cracking the ACT with DVD,
2010 Edition**
978-0-375-42960-6 • $31.99/C$39.99

**The Anxious Test-Taker's Guide to
Cracking Any Test**
978-0-375-42935-4 • $14.99/C$18.99

AP prep guides are available for
17 subjects. See a full title list at
PrincetonReview.com/bookstore

Fund It

**Paying for College Without
Going Broke, 2010 Edition**
978-0-375-42942-2 • $20.00/C$24.95

**Available online and in bookstores everywhere.
Find out more at PrincetonReview.com/Bookstore**